Greatest Fathers of the Church

An Introduction

Their Lives and Writings from AD 100 to AD 444

Lord of History Series
Volume II

ROBERT M. HADDAD

Greatest Fathers

Dedication

In honor
of those who acknowledge
Jesus Christ
as Lord of History

"It was his loving design, centered in Christ,
to give history its fulfilment by resuming everything in him,
all that is in heaven, all that is on earth,
summed up in him"
(Eph. 1:9-10).

Foreword

The fathers of the Second Vatican Council called for a "return to the authentic sources" as a well-spring from which guidance and wisdom could be drawn to assist in the great work of spreading the gospel of Christ in the modern world. In response to this call, there has been a renewed interest in early Church history, as well as the writings of the ancient Fathers of the Church. This has been evident particularly in the United States since the mid-1980s, as well as in other parts of the English-speaking world, including Australia.

The Church has had a long and chequered history. It is a history that is remote and unknown to most people today, including many Catholics. *The Lord of History Series* attempts to give an introduction to the early centuries of that history systematically through easy-to-read short chapters.

Volume I covers the first four centuries of Church history immediately following the period outlined in the *Acts of the Apostles*. It is an age of much drama, growth and suffering for the Church. There are many heroes, villains and controversies. We are introduced to the martyrs, saints and heroes who helped to expand the foundations of the Church, as well as the first great theologians, apologists and biblical exegetes. The Gospel of Christ is advancing, but in the face of official opposition and persecution. The various heresies are presented, together with the responses these elicited from the Church. The ultimate triumph of the Church is dealt with the chapters concerning the rise of Constantine, which are followed by a treatment of the great theological and Christological controversies of the fourth and fifth centuries. It is all stirring reading for the novice in Church history and a thorough introduction for those who want to pursue serious studies in this area.

Volume II is more specialised, looking at thirty of the most famous Fathers of the Church. The study of the Fathers is of perennial benefit to the Church and the faithful. These were men of undoubted sanctity and learning, whose writings contributed greatly to the authentic development of doctrine in those same early centuries. Many of the Fathers were also saints or martyrs, or even Doctors of the Church. Theirs is a wisdom that can never be dispensed with, a deep well from which new and old things can always be drawn. Again, in a simple and easy-to-read format, each chapter in this volume provides a basic biography of the Father in question, followed by a selection of individual quotes form their writings, carefully chosen to highlight the Catholic nature of their faith, and to illustrate that the early Church is the one same Holy Catholic Church we, by grace of God, belong to today.

George Cardinal Pell
Archbishop of Sydney   1 August 2003

Greatest Fathers

Index

1. Introduction — 1

THE APOSTOLIC FATHERS

2. The Didache — 4
3. St Clement of Rome — 8
4. St Ignatius of Antioch — 12
5. St Polycarp of Smyrna — 17
6. Papias — 22

FATHERS OF THE SECOND CENTURY

7. Aristides of Athens — 25
8. The Shepherd of Hermas — 28
9. St Justin Martyr — 31
10. Athenagoras of Athens — 36
11. St Theophilus of Antioch — 40
12. St Irenaeus of Lyons — 43

FATHERS OF THE THIRD CENTURY

13. Clement of Alexandria — 48
14. Tertullian — 53
15. St Hippolytus of Rome — 59
16. Origen — 63
17. St Cyprian of Carthage — 68
18. Lactantius — 73

NICENE AND POST NICENE FATHERS

19. St Athanasius of Alexandria	76
20. Eusebius Pamphilus of Caesarea	82
21. Didymus the Blind	86
22. St Cyril of Jerusalem	89
23. St Hilary of Poitiers	93
24. St Basil the Great	97
25. St Gregory Nazianzus	101
26. St Gregory of Nyssa	106
27. St Ambrose of Milan	110
28. St John Chrysostom	114
29. St Jerome	119
30. St Augustine of Hippo	123
31. St Cyril of Alexandria	132

Appendices

Appendix: The Fathers of the Church	137
Acknowledgments	139
About the Author	140
Other Works by the Author	141

Introduction

"On the other hand he who devotes himself to the study of the law of the Most High will seek out the wisdom of all the ancients ... he will preserve the discourse of notable men and penetrate the subtleties of parables" (Sir. 39:1-2).

This book is designed to study the earliest history of the Church with a particular view to discovering that it was Catholic from its very beginnings. In studying early Church history it is best to examine the *Fathers of the Church* and their writings. The study of the Fathers is called *Patrology*.

What is a *Father of the Church*? There are four determining tests:

(i) Orthodoxy
(ii) Sanctity
(iii) Antiquity
(iv) Church approval

Orthodoxy does not mean freedom from all *error*. In the writings of even the greatest Church Fathers one will find some error, however, with all true Church Fathers one always finds *a devotion to the Catholic Church and orthodox teaching*.

Sanctity implies that the particular Father was noted for his outstanding holiness according to Catholic morality in word and in deed.

Antiquity means that the Father lived and died between the years AD 100 and AD 749. The *Patristic Age* ended in the West in the year AD 636 with the death of St Isidore of Seville and in the East in the year AD 749 with the death of St John Damascene.

Church approval means that the Church has examined the writings of the Father in question and acknowledges their Catholic worth from all points of view – theological, philosophical, historical, etc. The Church has an official list of eighty-seven Fathers – forty-nine Greek and thirty-eight Latin (see Appendix A).

There is an enormous worth in studying the early Church Fathers for the purposes of Catholic *apologetics*. To best understand the teachings of Christ and the Apostles it is impossible to ignore the Fathers, particularly the *Apostolic Fathers*, as many of these actually knew and were taught directly by the Apostles themselves. Some of the greatest converts to Catholicism throughout the centuries attributed their conversion to their study of the Fathers — e.g., St Edmund Campion, Bl. John Henry Cardinal Newman. They saw that the Catholic Church was the Church of the first three centuries and that its main teachings can be found either explicitly or implicitly in the writings of this period.

Most anti-Catholic Protestants assert that the Catholic Church went "bad" after the victory of Constantine in AD 312. It was after this date that true evangelical Christianity was overrun by the Church of Rome, or *"Romanism"*, and that authentic Christianity was forced underground for over a thousand years until the true light of the Reformation broke out with the advent of Wycliffe, Luther, Calvin and co. "Romanism" as established by Constantine is a strange hybrid form of Christianity mixed with paganism imported from the ancient religions of Assyria, Babylon, Egypt, Persia, Greece and Rome. This view denies implicitly that the Church is a divine institution founded and protected by Christ (Mt 16:18-20), but rather is merely a human institution subject to the normal processes of birth, growth and decay.

What Protestants see in Catholicism that they cannot see in the New Testament is immediately labeled as "paganism" imported after Constantine. However, a study of the Fathers would reveal that such beliefs and practices in fact pre-date AD 312, are Apostolic in origin and are developments of Gospel truths rather than departures or inventions. Both Catholics and Protestants agree that this is the case with at least some doctrines — e.g., the Most Blessed Trinity. The Catholic Church is not an inventor of doctrine, but rather the divine depository of truth commissioned to expound and convey it from generation to generation free from all error.

Christ himself anticipated the development of doctrine:

"I have yet many things to say to you, but you cannot bear them now. When the Spirit of truth comes, he will guide you into all the truth; for he will not speak on his own authority, but whatever he hears he will speak, and he will declare to you the things that are to come" (Jn 16:12-13).

Introduction

Protestantism has cut itself off from history, the Fathers and Sacred Tradition through its insistence on *Sola Scriptura* (the Bible alone) and private interpretation. According to Newman, Protestantism was compelled to adopt *Sola Scriptura* because the Bible in the context of history, the Fathers and Tradition is not Protestantism. Effectively, therefore, the period from the death of St John the Apostle (AD 98-99) to Martin Luther (1517) is irrelevant to Protestant Christianity, hence their insistence on "the Book of Acts and nothing else." The reality is that without history one cannot have the Bible for it is history itself that tells us that the canon of the Bible was determined by the decrees of Popes St Damasus (AD 382) and St Innocent I (AD 405) and the decisions of the Councils of Hippo (AD 393) and Carthage (AD 397) which accepted as canonical the Greek Septuagint and all the books of the New Testament.

> "The Christianity of history is not Protestantism. If ever there was a safe truth it is this, and Protestantism has ever felt it so. To be deep in history is to cease to be a Protestant."
> (Cardinal Newman – An *Essay on the Development of Christian Doctrine*)

"The way of a fool is right in his own eyes, but a wise man listens to advice" (Prov. 12:15). A large part of the chaos in Christianity today is due to the Protestant notion of self-interpretation of the Bible. Those possessing this mentality cut themselves off from the accumulated wisdom of the past and become a theological law unto themselves. Western Christendom has ended up with as many divisions as private opinions. There is a wisdom, a wealth and a truth in the early Fathers which serves as a corrective leading to balanced and orientated Christianity.

Let us seek out the wisdom of the ancients through a study of the Fathers.

THE APOSTOLIC FATHERS

The Didache

(inter AD 90–150)

Historical Note

The Didache, or *Teaching of the Twelve Apostles*, is of undoubted antiquity and integrity. It is the belief of many Patrologists that this document was in use in the early Church even during the lifetime of St John the Evangelist: "*... many scholars would date the Didache to a point somewhere in the latter half of the first century, earlier, that is, than much of the New Testament itself.*" (Andrew Louth, *Early Christian Writers*, Penguin Books, 1968, p. 189). Other scholars are unwilling to give it a date earlier than the mid-second century AD.

The Didache is the earliest known catechism in the Church. It was used to instruct catechumens and neophytes well into the fourth century: "*Appointed by the Fathers to be read by those who newly joined, and who wish for instruction in the word of godliness ... that which is the 'Teaching of the Apostles'*" (St Athanasius, *Festal Letter* 39).

The contents of the Didache fall into two distinct divisions. The first part, or *The Two Ways*, provides an outline of Christian morality, virtues and vices under the headings of the Way of Life and the Way of Death; the second part sets out regulations dealing with Church worship with regard to baptism, fasting, the Eucharist, missionaries, etc., as well as a final eschatological chapter.

The author of the Didache remains a mystery. Some scholars have inferred that it might have had its origins in Alexandria. Nevertheless, the consensus nowadays is that the Didache is a compilation of pre-Christian Jewish materials and the author's own alterations and additions.

The Didache in its full text had been lost for over fourteen centuries. It had been long known that such a work existed, being referred to by Clement of Alexandria (*Miscellanies* 1:20:100), Eusebius of Caesarea (*Ecclesiastical History* 3:25) and St Athanasius (*ibid.*). It was only rediscovered in 1873 in a Constantinople monastery by Philotheos Bryennios, Metropolitan of Nicomedia in the *Codex Hierosolymitanus* (1056). Since its rediscovery numerous parts of the Didache have been recognized in other works, particularly in chapter 7 of the Syrian *Apostolic Constitutions* dating from the fourth century. We now have complete ancient copies of the Didache in Greek and Georgian, and partial extant copies in Latin, Coptic, Ethiopic and Syriac.

The greatest value of the Didache lies in the old regulations that reflect the life of the early Church somewhere in the Middle East in the obscure period between the end of the Apostolic and the beginning of the sub-Apostolic ages. These regulations undoubtedly testify to the catholicity of the Christian Church from its root beginnings.

Extracts

1:1
"There are two ways, one of life and one of death: and great is the difference between the two ways. The way of life is this: first, you shall love God, who created you; second, your neighbor as yourself."

2:1
"The second commandment of the teaching: You shall not murder. You shall not commit adultery. You shall not seduce boys. You shall not commit fornication. You shall not steal. You shall not practice magic. You shall not use potions. You shall not procure abortion, nor destroy a newborn child. You shall not bear false witness. You shall not speak evil. You shall not bear malice."

4:14

"Confess your offenses in church, and do not go up to your prayer with an evil conscience. This is the way of life."

7:1

"Baptize thus: After the foregoing instructions, baptize in the name of the Father and of the Son, and of the Holy Spirit, in living water. If you have no living water, then baptize in other water; and if you are not able in cold, then in warm. If you have neither, pour water three times on the head, in the name of the Father, and of the Son, and of the Holy Spirit. Before the Baptism, let the one baptizing and the one to be baptized fast, as also any others who are able."

8:1

"Bless those who curse you, and pray for your enemies: fast for those who persecute you ... Do not let your fasts be with the hypocrites. They fast on Monday and Thursday; but you will fast on Wednesday and Friday."

8:2

"Do not pray as the hypocrites do, but as the Lord commanded in His gospel, you shall pray thus: Our Father who art in heaven, hallowed be thy name. Thy kingdom come, thy will be done on earth, as it is in heaven. Give us this day our daily bread, and forgive us our debts, as we also forgive our debtors. And lead us not into temptation, but deliver us from evil. For thine is the power and the glory forever. Pray thus three times a day."

9:1

"Let no one eat or drink of the Eucharist with you except those who have been baptized in the name of the Lord; for it was in reference to this that the Lord said: 'do not give that which is holy to dogs.'"

14:1

"Assemble on the Lord's day, and break bread and offer the Eucharist; But first make confession of your faults, so that your sacrifice may be a pure one ... For this is the offering of which the Lord has said, 'Everywhere and always bring me a sacrifice that is undefiled, for I am a great king, says the Lord and my name is the wonder of nations' (Mal. 1:11)."

16:3

"... then will appear the deceiver of the world as a Son of God. He will work signs and wonders and the world will be given over into his hands. He will do such wicked deeds as have not been done since the world began ... And then will appear the signs of the truth. First, the sign spread out in the heavens; second, the sign of the sound of the trumpet; the third, the resurrection of the dead. Not the resurrection of all men, but as it was said: 'The Lord will come, and all His saints with Him.' Then the world will see the Lord coming on the clouds of heaven."

St Clement of Rome

(Pope c. AD 92–101)

Historical Note

We are aware from the writings of Hegesippus, St Irenaeus of Lyons and Eusebius of Caesarea that St Clement was the third successor to St Peter as Bishop of Rome (after Linus and Cletus). The fact that he held such a position of authority is clearly evident in the opening address of his epistle whereby he makes an attempt to heal the ruptures in the Church of Corinth which resulted in insurrection against the bishop and presbyters and their deposition. St Clement in his epistle is deeply concerned with the sin of pride which he saw as responsible for the jealousy, strife and disorders racking the Corinthians.

St Clement wrote only one epistle which was held in very high esteem in the early Church: "*Clement has left us one recognized epistle, long and wonderful, which he composed in the name of the church of Rome ... in many churches this epistle was read aloud to the assembled worshippers in early days, as it is in our own*" (Eusebius, *Ecclesiastical History* 3:4:80). The *Apostolical Canons* of the sixth century actually includes St Clement's epistle in the New Testament canon. Some in the early Church held the opinion that St Clement also wrote the book of Hebrews or translated it into Greek. Extant ancient copies of St Clement's epistle exist in Greek, Syriac and Latin.

Most authorities date the composition of St Clement's epistle around AD 96-98 (Lightfoot, Harnack, Funk). This dating is based upon the opening words of the epistle's main text, "*Owing to the sudden and repeated calamities and misfortunes which have befallen us*", as referring to the persecution of the Emperor Domitian. However, Jurgens (Vol. 1, p. 7) prefers to give the year AD 80 for the epistle's date basing his view that (i) the "repeated calamities" in question rather refers to the eruption of Vesuvius which also caused fire and pestilence in Rome, (ii) there are very few New Testament references in the work and (iii) that the martyrdom of Sts. Peter and Paul are referred to as recent events.

St Irenaeus (*Against Heresies* 3:3) states that St Clement knew and worshipped with Sts Peter and Paul. Both Origen and Eusebius identify him as the Clement who collaborated with St Paul and mentioned in his Epistle to the Philippians (4:3), but this is doubted by all other authorities (Andrew Louth, *Early Christian Writers*, Penguin Books, 1968, p. 18). According to Tertullian (*The Demurrer Against the Heretics* 32, c. AD 199), it was St Peter who ordained him as presbyter and then bishop of the Church of Rome. Hence the enormous value of his epistle in understanding ancient Apostolic teaching, especially as concerns the Eucharist.

Of the life and death of St Clement very little is known. According to Rufinus (c. AD 400) St Clement is said to have died a martyr's death in exile around AD 100 at the order of the Emperor Trajan. His crimes allegedly relating to his preaching and miracles which converted thousands, including hundreds of high rank. He was thrown into the Black Sea with an iron anchor. Around AD 868, St Cyril, while in the Crimea to evangelize the Kazars, dug up some bones in a mound together with an anchor and had them translated to Rome whereupon they were deposited by Pope Adrian II in the high altar of the basilica of St Clement.

Extracts

Letter to the Corinthians (c. AD 96-98)

Address 1:1
"The Church of God which sojourns in Rome to the Church of God which sojourns in Corinth ... Owing to the sudden and repeated calamities and misfortunes which have befallen us, we must acknowledge that we have been somewhat tardy in turning our attention to the matters in dispute among you."

32:4
"We, therefore, who have been called by his will in Christ Jesus, are not justified by ourselves, neither by our wisdom or understanding or piety, nor by the works we have wrought in holiness of heart, but by the faith by which almighty God has justified all men from the beginning ... What,

then, shall we do, brethren? Shall we cease from good works, and shall we put an end to love? May the Master forbid that such should ever happen among us; rather, let us be eager to perform every good work earnestly and willingly."

36:1
"This is the way, beloved, in which we found our salvation, Jesus Christ, the High Priest of our offerings, the defender and helper of our weakness. Through Him we fix our gaze on the heights of heaven; through Him we see the reflection of the faultless and lofty countenance of God; through Him the eyes of our heart were opened; through Him our foolish and darkened understanding shoots up to the light; through Him the Master willed that we should taste of deathless knowledge; who, being the brightness of His majesty, is as much greater than the angels as the more glorious name which He has inherited."

40:1-5
"He has commanded the offerings and services to be celebrated, and not carelessly nor in disorder, but at fixed times and hours ... Those, then, who make their offerings at the appointed times, are acceptable and blessed; for they follow the laws of the Master and do not sin. To the high priest, indeed, proper ministrations are allotted, to the priests a proper place is appointed, and upon the levites their proper services are imposed. The layman is bound by the ordinances for the laity."

42:1
"The Apostles received the gospel for us from the Lord Jesus Christ; and Jesus Christ was sent from God. Christ, therefore, is from God, and the Apostles are from Christ. Both of these orderly arrangements, then, are by God's will. Receiving their instructions and being full of confidence on account of the resurrection of Our Lord Jesus Christ, and confirmed in faith by the word of God, they went forth in the complete assurance of the Holy Spirit, preaching the good news that the Kingdom of God is coming. Through countryside and city they preached; and they appointed their earliest converts, testing them by the spirit, to be the bishops and deacons of future believers. Nor was this a novelty: for bishops and deacons had

been written about a long time earlier. Indeed, Scripture somewhere says: 'I will set up their bishops in righteousness and their deacons in faith.'"

44:1-5

"Our Apostles knew through our Lord Jesus Christ that there would be strife for the office of bishop. For this reason, therefore, having received perfect foreknowledge, they appointed those who have already been mentioned, and afterwards added the further provision that, if they should die, other approved men should succeed to their ministry ... Our sin will not be small if we eject from the episcopate those who blamelessly and holily have offered its sacrifices. Blessed are those presbyters who have already finished their course, and who have obtained a fruitful and perfect release."

46:6

"Do we not have one God, one Christ, and one Spirit of Grace poured out upon us? And is there not one calling in Christ?"

57:1

"You, therefore, who laid the foundation of the rebellion, submit to the presbyters and be chastened to repentance, bending your knees in a spirit of humility."

58:2

"Accept our counsel, and you will have nothing to regret. For as God lives, and as the Lord Jesus Christ lives, and the Holy Spirit, and the faith and hope of the elect, as surely will he that humbly and with equanimity and without regret carries out the commandments and precepts given by God, be enrolled and chosen among the number of those who are being saved through Jesus Christ, through whom there is glory to Him forever and ever. Amen."

St Ignatius of Antioch

(+ inter AD 107–116)

Historical Note

St Ignatius Theophorus of Antioch was the second successor to the See of Antioch in Syria after St Peter and St Evodius. We know next to nothing about his origin, birth and early life. According to Eusebius (*Ecclesiastical History* 3:36), he was elevated to this see in AD 69. It is highly possible that in his earlier years St Ignatius knew and worshipped with Sts Peter and Paul as both spent considerable time in Antioch. Tradition holds that it was St Peter himself who ordained St Ignatius a bishop: *"... he obtained this office from those saints, and that the hands of the blessed apostles touched his sacred head"* (Chrysostom, *Homilies on St Ignatius and St Babylas*, 9:136).

In his later years, St Ignatius became a disciple of the Apostle John and good friends with St Polycarp of Smyrna. Somewhere between AD 107-116, during the persecution of the Emperor Trajan, St Ignatius, by now an elderly man, was arrested and chained by the Romans on the charge of being a Christian. He was marched across Asia Minor to be eaten alive by lions in the Colosseum: *"I am His wheat, ground fine by the lion's teeth to be made purest bread for Christ"* (*Epistle to the Romans* 4). Along the way he was greeted by delegations from the various churches that flocked to venerate the renowned spiritual father.

It was during his agonizing journey to Rome that St Ignatius composed his now famous seven epistles in Greek addressed to the Christian communities at Ephesus, Magnesia, Tralles, Rome, Philadelphia, Smyrna and a personal one to St Polycarp. The principal themes emerging from his epistles are the authority of the clergy, the hatred of heresy and division and the greatness of martyrdom. Docetists and Judaizers received his strongest criticisms.

At the time of his death St Ignatius was "at least thirty years a bishop, probably trained by the Apostle John, and was apparently at this time the most venerated living member of the whole Church" (W. Carroll,

The Founding of Christendom, Christendom Press, 1993, Vol. 1, p. 455). His death was the work of one moment and afterwards his bones were collected by his friends and returned to Antioch.

Due to St Ignatius' direct association with the Apostles themselves his writings are an invaluable testimony to the faith and practice of the Apostolic and immediate post-Apostolic Church. Up until the fifteenth century, fifteen epistles were attributed to St Ignatius, including ones addressed to the Virgin Mary and St John. However, later eight of these were recognized as spurious. The authenticity of the remaining Ignatian epistles was also long challenged by Protestants due to their clear presentation of an hierarchical and monarchical Church. Three versions of Ignatian epistles have circulated, known respectively as the longer, middle and shorter recensions. The authenticity of the middle recension of seven epistles has now been acknowledged by both Catholic and Protestant scholars including Lightfoot, Harnack, Zahn and Funk.

Extracts

Letter to the Ephesians (c. AD 110)

Address
"Ignatius, also called Theophorus, to the Church at Ephesus in Asia ... united and chosen through true suffering by the will of the Father in Jesus Christ our God ... There is one Physician, who is both flesh and spirit, born and not born, who is God in man, true life in death, born both of Mary and from God, first able to suffer and then unable to suffer, Jesus Christ our Lord ... For our God, Jesus Christ, was conceived by Mary in accord with God's plan: of the seed of David, it is true, but also of the Holy Spirit."

18:2
"For our God, Jesus Christ, was conceived by Mary in accord with God's plan: of the seed of David, it is true, but also of the Holy Spirit. He was born and baptized so that by His submission He might purify the water. The virginity of Mary, her giving birth, and also the death of the Lord, were hidden from the prince of this world: — three mysteries loudly proclaimed, but wrought in the silence of God."

Letter to the Magnesians (c. AD 110)

6:1
"Take care to do all things in harmony with God, with the bishop presiding in the place of God and with the presbyters in the place of the council of the Apostles, and with the deacons, who are most dear to me, entrusted with the business of Jesus Christ."

9:1
"If, then, those who walked in ancient customs came to a new hope, no longer sabbathing but living by the Lord's Day, on which we came to life through Him and through His death."

Letter to the Trallians (c. AD 110)

2:2
"It is necessary, therefore, — and such is your practice — that you do nothing without the bishop, and that you be subject also to the presbytery, as to the Apostles of Jesus Christ our hope, in whom we shall be found, if we live in Him. It is necessary also that the deacons, the dispensers of the mysteries of Jesus Christ, be in every way pleasing to all men. For they are not the deacons of food and drink, but servants of the Church of God."

3:1
"In like manner let everyone respect the deacons as they would respect Jesus Christ, and just as they respect the bishop as a type of the Father, and the presbyters as the council of God and college of Apostles. Without these, it cannot be called a Church."

Letter to the Romans (c. AD 110)

Address
"Ignatius, also called Theophorus, to the Church that has found mercy in the greatness of the Most High Father and in Jesus Christ, His only Son: to the Church beloved and enlightened after the love of Jesus Christ, our God, by the will of Him that has willed everything which is: to the Church also which holds the presidency in the place of the country of the Romans

... To those who are united in flesh and in spirit by every commandment of His, who are filled with the grace of God without wavering, and who are filtered clear of every foreign stain, I wish an alloyed joy in Jesus Christ, our God."

4:1
"I am writing to all the Churches and I enjoin all, that I am dying willingly for God's sake, if only you do not prevent it. I beg of you, do not do me an untimely kindness. Allow me to be eaten by the beasts, which are my way of reaching to God."

Letter to the Philadelphians (c. AD 110)

4:1
"Take care, then, to use one Eucharist, so that whatever you do, you do according to God: for there is one Flesh of Our Lord Jesus Christ, and one cup in the union of His Blood; one altar, as there is one bishop with the presbytery and my fellow servants, the deacons."

8:1
"I did my best as a man devoted to unity. But where there is division and anger, God does not dwell. The Lord, however, forgives all who repent, if their repentance leads to the unity of God and to the council of the bishop. I have faith in the grace of Jesus Christ; and He will remove from you every chain."

Letter to the Smyrnaeans (c. AD 110)

7:1
"They abstain from the Eucharist and from prayer, because they do not confess that the Eucharist is the Flesh of our Savior Jesus Christ, Flesh which suffered for our sins and which the Father, in His goodness, raised up again. They who deny the gift of God are perishing in their disputes."

8:1
"You must all follow the bishop as Jesus Christ follows the Father, and the presbytery as you would the Apostles. Reverence the deacons as you would

the command of God. Let no one do anything of concern to the Church without the bishop. Let that be considered a valid Eucharist which is celebrated by the bishop, or by one whom he appoints. Wherever the bishop appears, let the people be there; just as wherever Jesus Christ is, there is the Catholic Church. Nor is it permitted without the bishop either to baptize or to celebrate the agape."

Letter to Polycarp (c. AD 110)

5:2
"If anyone is able to remain continent, to the honor of the flesh of the Lord, let him so remain without boasting."

St Polycarp of Smyrna

(c. AD 69/70–155/56)

Historical Note

Like St Ignatius of Antioch, St Polycarp of Smyrna was also a disciple of St John the Apostle and was conversant with many who had beheld Christ: *"He was instructed by Apostles, and had had familiar intercourse with many who had seen Christ"* (St Irenaeus of Lyons, Against Heresies 3:3:4, AD 180). This is the same Polycarp to whom St Ignatius addressed one of his epistles.

We know some details of the life of St Polycarp through his pupil St Irenaeus of Lyons. St Polycarp was born of Christian parents and hence was a believer in Christ from his childhood. He was considered a father figure in the Church of Asia Minor. Tertullian states that it was St John who appointed him to the see of Smyrna (*The Demurrer Against the Heretics* 32, c. AD 199). Some months before his arrest, St Polycarp visited Rome and met Pope Anicetus to discuss their differences regarding the time for observing Easter. They agreed to disagree and parted amicably after con-celebrating Mass.

St Polycarp died a martyr's death with eleven other Christians at the age of eighty-six in AD 155 after being exposed to wild beasts, fire and a knife, the knife being thrust only after the flames miraculously did not consume him: *"I myself saw him in my early years, for he lived a long time and was very old indeed when he laid down his life by a glorious and most splendid martyrdom"* (St Irenaeus of Lyons, Against Heresies, ibid.). St Polycarp's long life links the teachers and theologians of the mid-second century to the Apostolic founders of the Church.

St Polycarp wrote many letters, however, all that remains extant is his *Letter to the Philippians*, which is actually a composite of two letters written c. AD 110 and 135 respectively. The Philippians had expressed a desire to receive spiritual advice from St Polycarp so he responded with earnest warnings against the love of money and the Docetist heresy. In addition, there are instructions on the proper duties of presbyters and deacons as well as lay men and women.

St Polycarp was not an original writer but was steadfast in passing on the Apostolic truths he learned in his youth. He had a simple pious sense of the faith and reacted instinctively against any form of heresy. In his later years he was pained to see the widespread growth of false doctrine and cried out, *"O good God, what sort of era have you preserved me for, that I have to suffer such things as this!"* (Eusebius, *Eccl. History* 5:20).

After the death of St Polycarp, his faithful congregation in Smyrna was asked to give a full outline of the event. One of the actual witnesses, a certain Marcion, accordingly compiled what is now acknowledged as the earliest authentic record of a Christian martyrdom. *The Martyrdom of Polycarp* is written in a true story-teller's style and graphically describes the bishop's arrest and execution, making the reader feel part of the unfolding drama. This work became the model for the many pious martyrologies of the subsequent second and third centuries.

Extracts

The Letter(s) to the Philippians (c. AD 135)

3:1
"These things, brethren, concerning righteousness, I write to you not at my own instance, but because you first invited me."

4:2
"After that we can go on to instruct our womenfolk in the traditions of the faith, and in love and purity; teaching them to show fondness and fidelity to their husbands."

5:2
"Our duty, therefore, is to give everything of this kind a very wide berth, and be as obedient to our clergy and deacons as we should be to God and Christ."

6:1
"Let the presbyters be compassionate, merciful to all, bringing back those who have wandered astray, visiting those who are sick, neglecting neither widow nor orphan nor the poor, but providing always what is good in the sight of God and of men. Let them refrain entirely from anger, respect of persons, and unjust judgment; let them be far from the love of money, not quick to believe evil of anyone, not hasty in judgment, knowing that we are all debtors in the matter of sin."

7:1
"Everyone who does not confess that Jesus Christ has come in the flesh is an Antichrist; whoever does not confess the testimony of the cross, is of the devil; and whoever perverts the sayings of the Lord for his own desires, and says that there is neither resurrection nor judgment, such a one is the first-born of Satan."

The Martyrdom of St Polycarp (c. AD 155-157)

Address
"The Church of God which sojourns in Smyrna, to the Church of God which sojourns in Philomelium, and to all the dioceses of the holy and Catholic Church in every place."

8:1
"When finally he had finished his prayer, in which he remembered everyone with whom he had ever been acquainted, the small and the great, the renowned and the unknown, and the whole Catholic Church throughout the world, and the moment of departure had arrived, they seated him on an ass and led him into the city. It was the great Sabbath."

9:3
"When the Proconsul urged him and said, 'Take the oath and I will release you; revile Christ,' Polycarp answered: 'Eighty-six years I have served him, and He has never done me wrong. How, then, should I be able to blaspheme my King who has saved me.'"

12:2

"That teacher of Asia! That father-figure of the Christians! That destroyer of our gods!"

14:3

"In this way and for all things I do praise you, I do bless you, I do glorify you through the eternal and heavenly High Priest Jesus Christ, your beloved child: through whom be glory to you with Him and with the Holy Spirit, both now and through ages yet to come. Amen."

15:1; 16

"And then we who were privileged to witness it saw a wondrous sight; and we have been spared to tell it to the rest of you. The fire took on the shape of a hollow chamber, like a ship's sail when the wind fills it, and formed a wall round about the martyr's figure; and there was in the center of it, not like a human being in flames but like a loaf baking in the oven, or like a gold or silver ingot being refined in the furnace. And we became aware of a delicious fragrance, like the odor of incense or other precious gums ... Finally, when they realized that his body could not be destroyed by fire, the ruffians ordered one of the dagger-men to go up and stab him with his weapon."

17:3

"Christ we worship as the Son of God, but the martyrs we love as disciples and imitators of the Lord; and rightly so, because of their unsurpassable devotion to their own King and Teacher. With them may we also become companions and fellow disciples. When the centurion saw the contentiousness caused by the Jews, he confiscated the body, and, according to their custom, burned it. Then, at least, we took up his bones, more precious than costly gems and finer than gold, and put them in a suitable place. The Lord will permit us, when we are able, to assemble there in joy and gladness, and to celebrate the birthday of his martyrdom, both in memory of those who have already engaged in the contest, and for the practice and training of those who have yet to fight."

19:1

"He was not only a famous teacher, but also an outstanding witness, whose martyrdom all desire to imitate, because it was so much in accord with the gospel of Christ ... Now with the Apostles and all the just he is glorifying God and the Father Almighty, and he is blessing our Lord Jesus Christ, the Savior of our souls, the Helmsman of our bodies, and the Shepherd of the Catholic Church throughout the world."

St Papias

(inter AD 60–130)

Historical Note

What we know of St Papias is gathered from St Irenaeus and Eusebius. He was bishop of Hierapolis in Phrygia, east of Ephesus, and a friend of St Polycarp. According to St Irenaeus, St Papias was also a hearer of St John the Apostle: *"Papias, the hearer of John, and a companion of Polycarp, in his fourth book ..."* (*Against Heresies* 5:33:4). Others suggest that the same Apostle may have even ordained him bishop. However, critics have debated whether the John, whose disciple he was, was the Apostle John or a presbyter of the same name. Eusebius (*Ecclesiastical History* 3:39:2) points out that Papias himself states in his *Explanation* that he was only a hearer of acquaintances of the Apostles, therefore placing him among the third generation of Christians. Eusebius had little regard for St Papias, saying that he was "a man of very little intelligence." Later writers state that he was martyred in Rome.

We possess only one work composed by St Papias, the *"Explanation of the Sayings of the Lord."* Critics assign the composition of this work anywhere between AD 125-160. Originally in five volumes, we now only possess a few tiny fragments preserved by St Irenaeus, Eusebius and Apollinaris. No other writings of St Papias have come to light.

The *Explanation* attempts to explain both the words of Christ as well as His life. St Papias treats sayings of Christ from the Gospel, special utterances and parables from oral tradition, and stories that are pure fable. The latter include graphic descriptions of the millennium of which St Papias was an enthusiastic believer.

These sayings, utterances or stories were learned by St Papias from *"the presbyters."* This name may apply to the Apostles themselves or more probably to their immediate disciples. The presbyters lived generally between AD 70 and 150. Very few of them wrote anything of worth, their accounts and teachings being regarded as oral traditions.

Extracts

Fragments in Eusebius, *Ecclesiastical History*

3:39:1

"Of Papias there are five books in circulation, which bear the title Explanation of the Sayings of the Lord. Irenaeus remarks on these as the only ones written by him, writing very much as follows: 'These things, too, Papias, a man of ancient times, who was a hearer of John and a companion of Polycarp, attests in writing in the fourth of his books. He wrote five books.'"

3:39:2

"So much for Irenaeus. Papias himself, however, in the introduction to his treatises, makes it clear that he was never a hearer or an eyewitness of the Apostles. He shows, in fact, by the language he uses, that he received the doctrines of the faith through acquaintances of the apostles."

3:39:3

"I shall not hesitate to set down for you along with my interpretations whatever I learned from the presbyters and recall clearly, being thoroughly confident of their truth. Unlike most people, I do not delight in those who talk a great deal, but in those who teach the truth; nor in those who relate the commandments of others, but in those who relate the commandments given by the Lord to the faith, and which are derived from Truth itself."

3:39:4

"And then too, when anyone came along who had been a follower of the presbyters, I would inquire about the presbyters' discourses: what was said by Andrew, or by Peter, or by Philip, or by Thomas or James, or by John or Matthew, or by any other of the Lord's disciples: and what Aristion and the Presbyter John, the disciples of the Lord, say. It did not seem to me that I could get so much profit from the contents of books as from a living and abiding voice."

3:39:5
"Here it is worth noting that he twice mentions the name John: the first in connection with Peter and James and Matthew and the rest of the Apostles, clearly referring to the evangelist; but the other John he mentions after an interval, and groups him with others outside the number of the Apostles, placing Aristion before him; and he distinctly calls him a presbyter."

3:39:6
"In this way he makes it quite evident that their statement is true, who say that there were in Asia two persons of that name; and that there are in Ephesus two tombs, each of which even to the present time is called the tomb of John. It is important to take note of this: because if anyone would prefer the first, then probably it was the second who saw the Revelation which bears the name of John."

3:39:15
"And the Presbyter said this also: 'When Mark became the interpreter of Peter, he wrote down accurately whatever he remembered, though not in order, of the words and deeds of the Lord. He was neither hearer nor follower of the Lord; but such he was afterwards, as I say, of Peter, who had no intention of giving a connected account of the sayings of the Lord, but adapted his instructions as was necessary. Mark, then, made no mistake, but wrote things down as he remembered them; and he made it his concern to omit nothing that he had heard nor to falsify anything therein.' Such, then, is the account concerning Mark."

3:39:16
"In regard to Matthew, he says this: 'Matthew, indeed, composed the sayings in the Hebrew language; and each one interpreted them to the best of his ability.' The same writer made use of testimonies from the First Epistle of John, and likewise from that of Peter. And he related another story about a woman accused of many sins, which is contained in the Gospel of the Hebrews."

FATHERS OF THE SECOND CENTURY

Aristides of Athens

(c. AD 140)

Historical Note

According to Eusebius, Aristides was an Athenian philosopher who was "a man of faith and devoted to our religion." Besides this, we know next to nothing of him. His work *To Emperor Hadrian Caesar from the Athenian Philosopher Aristides* is the oldest complete apologetical text we possess (that written by Quadratus a few years earlier has been almost entirely lost).

For many centuries Aristides' apology had also been considered almost entirely lost with only a small Armenian fragment bearing the name of his work in our possession. Only in 1889 was a complete Syriac text rediscovered. Upon discovery of this Syriac text it was soon realised that a complete Greek text had always been extant as chapters 26 and 27 of a religious novel entitled *Barlaam and Josaphat* (author unknown).

The contents of Aristides' apology examine the beliefs of the four classes of men that comprise humanity – barbarians, Greeks, Jews and Christians. Only the Christians have the true conception and worship of God and lead lives worthy of Him. God must be eternal, impassible and perfect. The existence and order of the world proves the existence of such a God. The barbarians and Greeks worship the elements, famous men or gods that are slaves to passion; the Jews have only a child-like worship of the true God. Therefore, Rome should cease persecuting the Christians and convert to their religion.

Jurgens suggests (Vol. 1, p. 48) that Aristides' apology was actually addressed to the Emperor Antoninus Pius (Aelius Hadrianus Antoninus Pius) rather than the Emperor Hadrian (Publius Aelius Nerva Trajanus Hadrianus) in the early years of his reign (c. AD 140).

Extracts

Apology to the Emperor Hadrian Caesar (c. AD 140)

1
"When I saw that the world and all that is in it is moved by a force, I understood that He who moves and maintains it is God; for whatever moves something is stronger than that which is moved, and whatever maintains something is stronger than that which is maintained. I call the One who constructed all things and maintains them God: He that is without beginning and eternal, immortal and lacking nothing, and who is above all passions and failings such as anger and forgetfulness and ignorance and the rest."

4
"Let us proceed, then, O King, to the elements themselves, so that we may demonstrate concerning them that they are not gods, but corruptible and changeable things, produced out of the non-existent by Him that is truly God, who is incorruptible and unchangeable and invisible, but who sees all things and changes them and alters them as He wills."

15
"Christians trace their origin to the Lord Jesus Christ. He that came down from heaven in the Holy Spirit for the salvation of men is confessed to be the Son of the Most High God. He was born of a holy Virgin without seed of man, and took flesh without defilement; and He appeared among men so that He might recall them from the error of polytheism. When He had accomplished His wonderful design, by His own free will and for a mighty purpose He tasted of death on the cross. After three days, however, He came to life again and went up into the heavens.

It is possible for you, O king, to learn to know the report of His coming in the holy gospel writing, as it is called by us - should you chance to come upon a copy. He had twelve disciples who, after His ascent into the heavens, went out into the provinces of the world teaching about His greatness. In this way one of them came through the places around about us, announcing the doctrine of truth. Since then, they who continue to observe the righteousness which was preached by His disciples are called Christians. These are they who, above every people of the earth, have found the truth; for they acknowledge God, the Creator and Maker of all things, in the only-begotten Son and in the Holy Spirit.

Other than Him, no god do they worship. They have the commandments of the Lord Jesus Christ Himself impressed upon their hearts, and they observe them, awaiting the resurrection of the dead and the life of the world to come. They do not commit adultery nor fornication, nor do they bear false witness, nor covet the goods of other men. They honor father and mother and love their neighbors; and they render just judgment. What they would not want done to them, they do not do to another. They make appeal to those who wrong them, and win them to themselves as friends.

They hasten to do good to their enemies. They are gentle and reasonable. They abstain from every unlawful exchange and from all uncleanness. They despise not the widow, nor do they distress the orphan. Whoever has, distributes liberally to him that has not. Should they see a stranger, they take him under roof, and rejoice over him as over a blood brother. For not after the flesh do they call themselves brethren, but after the spirit. For the sake of Christ they are ready to lay down their lives. They keep His commands without wavering, living holy and just lives as the Lord God commanded them; and they give thanks to Him every hour for all their food and drink and for the rest of their goods.

The Shepherd of Hermas

(inter AD 140–155)

Historical Note

It is stated in the anonymous *Muratorian Fragment* (inter AD 155-200) that the author of *The Shepherd* was Hermas, the brother of St Pius I who sat on the See of Peter from c. AD 140-155. According to his autobiography, Hermas claimed to be a contemporary of St Clement of Rome.

Hermas was originally a slave who later became a freedman after being sold to a Christian. He then applied himself to business and farming amassing great wealth. Consequently, he neglected his spiritual life and, more particularly, failed to morally guide his wife and children. When persecution came, however, he and his wife confessed the faith only to be betrayed by their apostate children. Hermas' betrayal resulted in the loss of his fortune but led to his conversion to fervor. It was while endeavoring to do penance for the past that he composed *The Shepherd*.

The Shepherd was apparently written in Rome. What are still possessed of it are two Greek manuscripts, both incomplete, two ancient Latin texts, an Ethiopic version and fragments of a Coptic version. St Irenaeus, Tertullian, Clement of Alexandria and Origen considered it an inspired work of a true prophet, though not a canonical work. It was often appended to New Testament manuscripts, however, dwindled in popularity from the fourth century onwards. The decree of Pope Gelasius (AD 496) listed it among the apocryphal books.

The purpose of *The Shepherd* was to call clergy and laity responsible for grave disorders in the Roman Church to penance. The necessity of penance, its efficacy and its conditions form the groundwork of the work.

Hermas presents his ideas as a seer passing on visions and revelations that have been given to him. This was done so that his readers would more readily accept his ideas. There are two distinct personages who appear to Hermas. The first is the Church in the form of an aged woman who grows younger and more graceful with each vision; the second is the Angel of Penance to whose care Hermas has been entrusted.

The *Shepherd* is divided into three parts, namely, five *Visions*, twelve *Commandments*, and ten *Parables*. Together, they insist upon virtues and good works, faith, fear of the Lord, chastity, simplicity, patience, temperance, truthfulness, and the discernment of prophets. Hermas possessed the qualities of an excellent moralist with a deep sense of divine mercy. His work achieved a great deal of good in the early centuries.

Extracts

Vis. 2:2:1
"After fifteen days during which I fasted and prayed much to the Lord, the knowledge of the writing was revealed to me."

Vis. 2:4:3
"Therefore shall you write two little books and send one to Clement and one to Grapte. Clement shall then send it to the cities abroad, because that is his duty; and Grapte shall instruct the widows and the orphans. But you shall read it in this city along with the presbyters who are in charge of the Church."

Mand. 4:1:4
"What then, sir," said I, "shall the husband do, if the wife continue in this disposition? (i.e., adultery)." "Let him divorce her", he said, "and let the husband remain single. But if he divorce his wife and marry another, he too commits adultery." "If, then, sir," said I, "after the wife be divorced, she repent and wish to return to her own husband, is she not to be received?" "Indeed", he said, "if the husband does not receive her, he sins and brings great sin upon himself. It is necessary, in fact, to receive the sinner who repents."

Par. 5:3:2
"Thus, then, shall you observe the fasting which you intend to keep. First of all, be on your guard against every evil word, and every evil desire, and purify your heart from all the vanities of this world. If you guard against

these things, your fasting will be perfect. And you will do also as follows. Having fulfilled what is written, in the day on which you fast you will taste nothing but bread and water; and having reckoned up the price of the dishes of that day which you intended to have eaten, you will give it to a widow, or an orphan, or to some person in want, and thus you will exhibit humility of mind, so that he who has received benefit from your humility may fill his own soul, and pray for you to the Lord. If you observe fasting, as I have commanded you, your sacrifice will be acceptable to God, and this fasting will be written down; and the service thus performed is noble, and sacred, and acceptable to the Lord."

Par. 5:6:2
"God planted the vineyard, (the shepherd) said: that is, He created the people, and gave them over to His Son. And the Son appointed the angels to guard over them; and He Himself cleansed them of their sins, laboring much and undergoing much toil."

Par. 9:16:2
"They had need to come up through the water, so that they might be made alive; for they could not otherwise enter into the Kingdom of God except by putting away the mortality of their former life. These also, then, who had fallen asleep received the seal of the Son of God, and entered into the Kingdom of God. For before a man bears the name of the Son of God, he is dead. But when he receives the seal, he puts mortality aside and again receives life. The seal, therefore, is the water. They go down into the water dead, and come out of it alive."

Par. 9:31:4
"But I say to you, as many as have received the seal: maintain your innocence, bear no grudge, do not persist in wickedness nor in the bitter memory of past offenses. Be of one spirit and put away these wicked divisions. Remove them from your midst, so that the Master of the flock may rejoice in His sheep. He will rejoice if all be found whole. But if He find some of them fallen away, woe to the shepherds. And if the shepherds themselves be fallen away, how shall they answer for the flock?"

St Justin Martyr

(c. AD 100–165)

Historical Note

St Justin Martyr was the first of the outstanding apologists of the Church and the greatest of the second century. He was born of pagan parents in Flavia Neapolis (Palestine) some time after AD 100. St Justin embraced Christianity around AD 130 after being a Stoic, Peripatetic, Pythagorean and Platonist.

We know of St Justin's life mostly through his own writings. He was a prolific writer and itinerant Christian philosopher defending the teaching of Christ as the highest and most perfect philosophy. He was the first to study the relation between faith and reason and introduced Greek philosophical terminology into his expositions.

He was admired for his earnest convictions, noble character and perfect loyalty in his dealings. He was an apostle and saint in the true sense of the words. After spending time teaching in Ephesus, St Justin moved to Rome and there set up a successful Christian school, having Tatian the Syrian as one of his students.

Of all his writings only three have survived substantially intact, namely his two *Apologies* and the *Dialogue with Trypho the Jew*. St Justin wrote his apologies to the Emperor Antoninus Pius, his adopted sons and to the Roman Senate explaining and defending Christian faith and practice. In his works we find the first open written account of the Christian mysteries, particularly baptism and the Eucharist, hitherto kept under wraps by the "discipline of the secret."

St Justin wrote convincingly to dispel the widely spread calumnies that Christians were atheists, cannibals and sexually immoral. The Christians were not only moral but also loyal to all legitimate authority and therefore deserving of tolerance: "And if these things seem to you to be *reasonable and true, honor them; but if they seem nonsensical, despise them as nonsense, and do not decree death against those who have done no wrong, as you would enemies*" (*First Apology* 68). Christians were persecuted only out of ignorance and misapprehension, stirred on by the demons. Unfortunately, St Justin's hope of getting the Emperor to repeal the anti-Christian laws had no effect.

The *Dialogue with Trypho the Jew* is the oldest known apologetical work against Judaism. Trypho was probably a historical person, a learned Rabbi of some note who openly debated with St Justin at Ephesus between AD 132-135. The *Dialogue* was written around AD 155 as a record of the disputation which lasted two days.

There exist also four fragments of another treatise entitled *On the Resurrection*. Various patristic writers ascribe this work to St Justin, including St John Damascene. Whether or not it is an authentic work of St Justin it is undoubtedly ancient, being alluded to by Methodius of Olympus at the end of the third century.

According to the authentic *Martyrdom of Sts Justin and Sociorum*, St Justin and six companions were denounced to the authorities as Christians in AD 165, perhaps by the cynic Crescens. After being tried and condemned by the Prefect Junius Rusticus, all seven were scourged and beheaded by sword. Eusebius referred to St Justin as "an ornament of our Faith soon after the Apostles' time" (*Ecclesiastical History* 2:13).

Extracts

First Apology to the Emperor Antoninus Pius (inter AD 148-155)

13
"Our teacher of these things, born for this end, is Jesus Christ, who was crucified under Pontius Pilate, the procurator in Judea in the time of Tiberius Caesar. We will prove that we worship Him reasonably; for we have learned that He is the Son of the True God Himself, that He holds a second place, and the spirit of Prophecy a third. For this they accuse us of madness, saying that we attribute to a crucified man a place second to the unchangeable and eternal God, the Creator of all things; but they are ignorant of the mystery which lies therein."

15

"According to our Teacher, just as they are sinners who contract a second marriage, even though it be in accord with human law, so also are they sinners who look with lustful desire at a woman. He repudiates not only one who actually commits adultery, but even one who wishes to do so; for not only our actions are manifest to God, but even our thoughts."

61

"As many as are persuaded and believe that what we teach and say is true, and undertake to be able to live accordingly, are instructed to pray and to entreat God with fasting, for the remission of their sins that are past, we praying and fasting with them. Then they are led by us to a place where there is water; and there they are reborn in the same kind of rebirth in which we ourselves were reborn: in the name of God, the Lord and Father of all and of our Savior, Jesus Christ, and of the Holy Spirit, they receive the washing with water. For Christ said, 'unless you be reborn, you shall not enter into the Kingdom of Heaven ...' The reason for doing this, we have learned from the Apostles ... in order that we may not remain the children of necessity ... and may obtain in the water the remission of sins formerly committed."

66

"And this food is called among us the Eucharist, of which no one is allowed to partake but the man who has been washed in the washing bath that is for the remission of sins, and unto regeneration, and who is so living as Christ has enjoined. For not as common bread nor common drink do we receive these; but since Jesus Christ our Savior was made incarnate by the word of God and had both flesh and blood for our salvation, so too, as we have been taught, the food which has been made into the Eucharist by the Eucharistic prayer set down by Him, and by the change of which our blood and flesh is nourished is both the flesh and the blood of that incarnated Jesus ... The Apostles, in the Memoirs which they produced, which are called Gospels, have thus passed on that which was enjoined upon them: that Jesus took bread and, having given thanks, said, 'Do this in remembrance of Me; this is My Body.' And in like manner, taking the cup, and having given thanks, He said, 'This is My Blood.' And He imparted this to them only."

67

"And on the day called Sunday, all who live in the cities or in the country gather together to one place and the memoirs of the apostles or the writings of the prophets are read, as long as time permits; then, when the reader has ceased, the president verbally instructs, and exhorts to the imitation of these good things. Then we all rise together and pray, and, as we before said, when our prayer is ended bread and wine are brought, and the president in like manner offers prayers and thanksgivings, according to his ability, and the people assent, saying, Amen; and there is a distribution to each and a participation of that over which thanks have been given and to those who are absent a portion is sent by the deacons."

Dialogue with Trypho the Jew (c. AD 155)

10

"Is there any other matter, my friends, in which we are blamed? ... Are our lives and customs also slandered by you? And I ask this: have you also believed concerning us, that we eat men, and that after the feast, having extinguished the lights, we engage in promiscuous concubinage?"

23

"If circumcision was not necessary before Abraham, nor before Moses the Sabbath observance and festivals and sacrifices, then, similarly they are not necessary now, when in accordance with the will of God, Jesus Christ the Son of God has been born without sin, of a Virgin of the offspring of Abraham."

41

"Hence God speaks by the mouth of Malachi, one of the twelve prophets, as I said before, about the sacrifices at that time presented by you: 'I have no pleasure in you,' says the Lord, 'and I will not accept your sacrifices at your hands; for, from the rising of the sun to the going down of the same, My Name has been glorified among the Gentiles, and in every place incense is offered to My name, and a pure offering: for My Name is great among the Gentiles says the Lord, but you profane it.' He then speaks to those Gentiles, namely us, who in every place offer sacrifices to Him, i.e., the bread of the Eucharist, and also the cup of the Eucharist, affirming both that we glorify His Name and you profane it."

100

"He became Man by the Virgin so that the course which was taken by disobedience in the beginning through the agency of the serpent, might be also the very course by which it would be put down. For Eve, a virgin and undefiled, conceived the word of the serpent, and bore disobedience and death. But the Virgin Mary received faith and joy when the angel Gabriel announced to her the glad tidings that the Spirit of the Lord would come upon her and the power of the Most High would overshadow her, for which reason the Holy One being born of her is the Son of God. And she replied: 'Be it done unto me according to thy word.'"

The Resurrection (date unknown)

8

"Indeed, God calls even the body to resurrection, and promises it everlasting life. When He promises to save the man, He thereby makes His promise to the flesh: for what is man but a rational living being composed of soul and body?"

Athenagoras of Athens

(+post AD 180)

Historical Note

Most of what we know about Athenagoras of Athens is the little he mentions of himself in his own writings. A passing reference to him is made by Methodius of Olympus in his treatise *The Resurrection*. Philip of Side in his *Christian History* (c. AD 430) mentions that he was born a heathen and became a Christian after reading the Scriptures. We have no details of his year of birth and length of life, but we are certain that he was a contemporary of St Justin Martyr and Tatian the Syrian. Nor do we know the manner of his death except that it took place shortly after AD 180.

Athenagoras was a Christian philosopher skilled in grammar, rhetoric and logic and possessed with forcible reasoning and a powerful style of Greek devoid of antagonism and insults. His primary object was to instruct and demonstrate. He never strays from his subject and is so concise that he verges at times on dryness.

His *Supplication for the Christians*, composed around AD 177, was addressed to the Emperor Marcus Aurelius and his son Commodus. It was an attempt to refute the widespread calumnies circulated by pagans that the Christians were atheists, cannibals and incestuous. Athenagoras refutes these calumnies successively: the Christians are not atheists for they worship one God, Father, Son and Holy Spirit; Christians are not sexually immoral, rather they fear hell and are condemned to there for even the thought of evil; and as for cannibalism, Christians hate homicide, avoid the gladiatorial fights, condemn abortion and infanticide and believe in the resurrection of the body. Athenagoras concludes with an appeal to Aurelius and Commodus for justice.

The Resurrection of the Dead is a philosophical work of Athenagoras written very shortly after the *Supplication* to prove the fact of a universal resurrection from natural reason. It was probably originally a lecture delivered orally and then circulated as a pamphlet.

Athenagoras draws no proof for the resurrection from Christian Tradition or the Scriptures. Many of the reasonings developed by subsequent philosophers in support of the resurrection can be found in this work. In the first part, Athenagoras proves that the resurrection of the body is not beyond the power of an omnipotent God. In the second part, he argues in favor of the unity of the human person both body and immortal soul, concluding that as the body participates in the good and bad actions of the soul it must likewise be rewarded or punished with it. This can only occur if there is a resurrection.

Extracts

Supplication for the Christians (c. AD 177)

1
"But for us who are called Christians you have not in like manner cared; but although we commit no wrong — nay, as will appear in the sequel of this discourse, are of all men most piously and righteously disposed towards the Deity and towards your government — you allow us to be harassed, plundered, and persecuted, the multitude making war upon us for our name alone."

3
"Three things are alleged against us: atheism, Thyestean feasts, Oedipodean intercourse. But if these charges are true, spare no class: proceed at once against our crimes; destroy us root and branch, with our wives and children, if any Christian is found to live like the brutes."

10
"That we are not atheists, therefore, seeing that we acknowledge one God, uncreated, eternal, invisible, impassible, incomprehensible, illimitable, who is apprehended by the understanding only and the reason, who is encompassed by light, and beauty, and spirit, and power ineffable, by whom the universe has been created through His Logos, and set in order, and is kept in being ... But the Son of God is the Logos of the Father, in idea and in operation; for after the pattern of Him and by Him were all things made, the Father and the Son being one. And, the Son being in the

Father and the Father in the Son, in oneness and power of spirit, the understanding and reason of the Father is the Son of God. The Holy Spirit also, who works in those who speak prophetically, we regard as an effluence of God, flowing out and returning like a ray of the sun. Who, then, would not be astonished to hear those called atheists, who speak of God the Father and of the Son and of the Holy Spirit, and who proclaim Their power in union and Their distinction in order?"

33

"Nay, you would find many among us, both men and women, growing old unmarried, in hope of living in closer communion with God. But if the remaining in virginity and in the state of an eunuch brings nearer to God, while the indulgence of carnal thought and desire leads away from Him, in those cases in which we shun the thoughts, much more do we reject the deeds."

35

"For when they know that we cannot endure even to see a man put to death, though justly; who of them can accuse us of murder or cannibalism? Who does not reckon among the things of greatest interest the contests of gladiators and wild beasts, especially those which are given by you? But we, deeming that to see a man put to death is much the same as killing him, have abjured such spectacles. How, then, when we do not even look on, lest we should contract guilt and pollution, can we put people to death? And when we say that those women who use drugs to bring on abortion commit murder, and will have to give an account to God for the abortion, on what principle should we commit murder? For it does not belong to the same person to regard the very foetus in the womb as a created being, and therefore an object of God's care."

The Resurrection of the Dead (inter AD 177-180)

12

"Thus the soul exists and continues unchanged in the nature in which it was made, and performs what is natural to it ... And the body is moved to what is proper to it in accord with its nature, and undergoes the changes allotted to it; and among the other changes of age, appearance and size, is the resurrection. For the resurrection is a species of change, the last of all, and a change for the better in those things which remain at that time."

15

"For if the whole nature of men in general is composed of an immortal soul and a body which was fitted to it in the creation, and if neither to the nature of the soul by itself, nor to the nature of the body separately, has God assigned such a creation or such a life and entire course of existence as this, but to men compounded of the two, in order that they may, when they have passed through their present existence, arrive at one common end."

St Theophilus of Antioch

(+ inter AD 185–191)

Historical Note

St Theophilus was the seventh bishop of Antioch and sixth successor to St Peter. Born a pagan near the Euphrates River in Syria he converted to Christianity after studying and meditating on the Scriptures. The only details we possess about his life are gathered from his *To Autolycus*, his only surviving work completed after the death of the Emperor Marcus Aurelius in AD 180.

St Theophilus received a Greek education and had some knowledge of Hebrew. Though limited in philosophical depth he was widely read and familiar with a variety of literary culture. In AD 169, he succeeded Cornelius to the see of Antioch. Eusebius dates the end of his episcopate in AD 177, but it was undoubtedly some years later.

To Autolycus is a major apologetical work in three volumes. They are in effect three separate books joined together for they are addressed to the same person and deal with the same topics. Autolycus was a learned pagan and magistrate. In the first volume, St Theophilus treats of the nature of the Christian God, extolling Him as the true God and denouncing the gods of paganism. In the second volume, the author exposes the inadequacy and puerileness of pagan teachings, contrasting them to the superior teachings found in the Holy Scriptures about the creation of the world, the worship due to God and authentic morality. The third volume refutes the calumnies brought against the Christians concerning incest and cannibalism and gives an outline of world history to show the antiquity of Judeo-Christian history and Scriptures compared to those of paganism.

St Theophilus wrote a number of other works that are now all lost. These include two books on the origin of humanity mentioned in *To Autolycus*, a work against the heresy of Hermogenes, another against the heresy of Marcion, a *Commentary on the Book of Proverbs*, *Commentaries on the Gospel*, and a number of smaller works for instruction and edification.

Extracts from the Scripture commentaries can be found in the writings of St Jerome. The other writings are mentioned by Eusebius (*Ecclesiastical History* 4:24). St Theophilus died sometime between AD 185 and 191.

Extracts

To Autolycus (AD 181)

1:12
"Are you unwilling to be anointed with the oil of God? It is on this account that we are called Christians: because we are anointed with the oil of God."

1:14
"But do you also, if you please, give reverential attention to the prophetic Scriptures, and they will make your way plainer for escaping the eternal punishments, and obtaining the eternal prizes of God. For He who gave the mouth for speech, and formed the ear to hear, and made the eye to see, will examine all things, and will judge righteous judgment, rendering merited awards to each. To those who by patient continuance in well-doing seek immortality, He will give life everlasting, joy, peace, rest, and abundance of good things, which neither hath eye seen, nor ear heard, nor hath it entered into the heart of man to conceive. But to the unbelieving and despisers, who obey not the truth, but are obedient to unrighteousness, when they shall have been filled with adulteries and fornications, and filthiness, and covetousness, and unlawful idolatries, there shall be anger and wrath, tribulation and anguish, and at the last everlasting fire shall possess such men."

2:15
"The three days before the luminaries were created are types of the Trinity: God, His Word, and His Wisdom."

2:16
"Moreover, those things which were created from the waters were blessed by God, so that this might also be a sign that men would at a future time

receive repentance and remission of sins through water and the bath of regeneration – all who proceed to the truth and are born again and receive a blessing from God."

2:22

"But what else is this voice but the Word of God, who is also His Son? Not as the poets and writers of myths talk of the sons of gods begotten from intercourse [with women], but as truth expounds, the Word, that always exists, residing within the heart of God. For before anything came into being He had Him as a counsellor, being His own mind and thought. But when God wished to make all that He determined on, He begot this Word, uttered, the first-born of all creation, not Himself being emptied of the Word [Reason], but having begotten Reason, and always conversing with His Reason. And hence the holy writings teach us, and all the spirit-bearing [inspired] men, one of whom, John, says, 'In the beginning was the Word, and the Word was with God,' showing that at first God was alone, and the Word in Him. Then he says, 'The Word was God; all things came into existence through Him; and apart from Him not one thing came into existence.' The Word, then, being God, and being naturally produced from God, whenever the Father of the universe wills, He sends Him to any place; and He, coming, is both heard and seen, being sent by Him, and is found in a place."

3:15

"But far be it from Christians to conceive any such deeds; for with them temperance dwells, self-restraint is practised, monogamy is observed, chastity is guarded, iniquity exterminated, sin extirpated, righteousness exercised, law administered, worship performed, God acknowledged: truth governs, grace guards, peace screens them; the holy word guides, wisdom teaches, life directs, God reigns."

St Irenaeus of Lyons

(c. AD 140–202)

Historical Note

St Irenaeus was born in Asia Minor around AD 140. He was probably a native of Smyrna where in his younger years he was acquainted with St Polycarp. During this time, he became an assiduous disciple of the aged bishop and would later appeal to his authority. Around AD 177-178, at only thirty-seven years of age, St Irenaeus became the second bishop of Lyons, succeeding the martyred St Pothinus. The reasons for such a radical move remain clouded in mystery.

St Irenaeus stands out in history for a number of important reasons: firstly, he was involved in trying to bring peace between Pope Victor I of Rome and Polycrates of Ephesus concerning the proper date for the celebration of Easter; secondly, he combated Gnosticism through his compiling of *Against Heresies*, a work which ranks him as certainly the most important theologian of the second century (Jurgens vol. 1, p. 84); thirdly, he labored zealously for the conversion of the countryside around Lyons.

The full name for *Against Heresies* is *The Detection and Overthrow of the Gnosis Falsely So-called*. This enormous five-volume work was originally written entirely in Greek between AD 180 and 199. Up until certain discoveries of Gnostic writings in the mid-1940's the *Against Heresies* was the primary source for knowledge of Gnostic beliefs.

St Irenaeus wrote *Against Heresies* at the request of a friend, perhaps a bishop, who desired an exposition of heresies he was unfamiliar with. The first volume deals with the detection of the errors of the various Gnostic sects, the second and fifth are devoted to refuting these errors. His exposition of the Gnostic systems is sincere and well informed. The third book outlines the rule of faith for Christians, which is the teaching of the Apostles preserved and passed on by the Church. The principles he established concerning the doctrinal authority of the Church, and of Rome in particular, amount also to a refutation in advance of future heresies. The fourth book contains arguments from both the Old and New

Testaments, with a confirmation of the divine origin of the Old Testament against the Marcionites.

Other works of St Irenaeus include the treatise *Demonstration of the Apostolic Teaching*, which contains an exposition and proof of the truth of principal Christian dogmas for the faithful; a letter *On the Monarchy of God* which contains the teachings of St Polycarp against God as the author of evil; and other letters, namely, *On the Ogdoad*, *On Schism*, *On Science*, and fragments contained in Eusebius (*Ecclesiastical History* 5:16; 19:1) of letters to Pope Victor on the Easter question.

After the incident between Pope Victor and Polycrates, St Irenaeus drops out of the limelight. According to Sts Jerome and Gregory of Tours, he died a martyr's death around AD 202 in the general massacres of Christians under Septimus Severus, though Eusebius, who possessed a good knowledge of St Irenaeus' life, makes no mention of this.

Extracts

Against Heresies (c. AD 180)

1:10:1
"For the Church, although dispersed throughout the whole world even to the ends of the earth, has received from the Apostles and from their disciples the faith in one God, Father Almighty, the Creator of heaven and earth and sea and all that is in them; and in one Jesus Christ, the Son of God who became flesh for our salvation; and in the Holy Spirit, who announced through the prophets the dispensations and the comings, and the birth from a Virgin, and the passion, and the resurrection from the dead, and the bodily ascension into heaven in the glory of the Father to re-establish all things; and the raising up again of all flesh of all humanity, in order that to Jesus Christ our Lord and God and Savior and King, in accord with the approval of the invisible Father, every knee shall bend of those in heaven and on earth and under the earth, and that every tongue shall confess Him, and that He may make just judgment of them all; and that He may send the spiritual forces of wickedness and the angels who transgressed and became apostates, and the impious, unjust, lawless and blasphemous amongst men, into everlasting fire; and that He may grant

life, immortality, and surround with eternal glory the just and the holy, and those who have kept His commands and who have persevered in His love, either from the beginning or from their repentance."

3:3:1

"When, therefore, we have such proofs, it is not necessary to seek among others the truth which is easily obtained from the Church. For the Apostles, like a rich man in a bank, deposited with her most copiously everything which pertains to the truth; and everyone whosoever wishes draws from her the drink of life. For she is the entrance to life, while all the rest are thieves and robbers. That is why it is surely necessary to avoid them, while cherishing with the utmost diligence the things pertaining to the Church, and to lay hold of the tradition of truth ... In the Church, God has placed apostles, prophets and doctors, and all the other means through which the Spirit works; in all of which none have any part who do not conform to the Church. On the contrary, they defraud themselves of life by their wicked opinion and most wretched behavior. For where the Church is, there is the Spirit of God; and where the Spirit of God, there the Church and every grace."

3:3:2

"The successions of the bishops of the greatest and most ancient Church known to all, founded and organized at Rome by the two most glorious Apostles, Peter and Paul, that Church which has the tradition and the faith which comes down to us after having been announced to men by the Apostles. For with this the whole world; and it is in her that the faithful everywhere have maintained the Apostolic tradition."

3:3:3

"The blessed Apostles (Peter and Paul), having founded and built up the Church (of Rome), they handed over the office of the episcopate to Linus. Paul makes mention of this Linus in the Epistle to Timothy. To him succeeded Anacletus; and after him, in the third place from the Apostles, Clement was chosen for the episcopate ... In this order, and by the teaching of the Apostles handed down in the Church, the preaching of the truth has come down to us."

3:4:1

"If there should be a dispute over some kind of question, ought we not have recourse to the most ancient Churches in which the Apostles were familiar, and draw from them what is clear and certain in regard to that question? What if the Apostles had not in fact left writings to us? Would it not be necessary to follow the order of tradition, which was handed down to those to whom they entrusted the Churches?"

3:19:1

"Nevertheless, what cannot be said of anyone else who ever lived, that He is Himself in His own right God and Lord and Eternal King and Only-begotten and Incarnate Word, proclaimed as such by all the Prophets and by the Apostles and by the Spirit Himself, may be seen by all who have attained to even a small portion of the truth. The Scriptures would not have borne witness to these things concerning Him, if, like everyone else, He were mere man."

3:22:4

"(Eve) having become disobedient, was made the cause of death for herself and for the whole human race; so also Mary, betrothed to a man but nevertheless still a virgin, being obedient, was made the cause of salvation for herself and for the whole human race ... Thus, the knot of Eve's disobedience was loosed by the obedience of Mary. What the virgin Eve had bound in unbelief, the Virgin Mary loosed through faith."

4:17:5

"He took that created thing, bread, and gave thanks and said, 'This is My Body.' And the cup likewise, which is part of that creation to which we belong, He confessed to be His Blood, and taught the new oblation of the new covenant, which the Church, receiving from the Apostles, offers to God throughout the world ... concerning which Malachy, among the twelve prophets thus spoke beforehand: 'From the rising of the sun to the going down, My name is glorified among the gentiles, and in every place incense is offered to My name and a pure sacrifice' ... indicating in the plainest manner that in every place sacrifice shall be offered to Him, and at that a pure one."

4:33:2
"If the Lord were from other than the Father, how could He rightly take bread, which is of the same creation as our own, and confess it to be His Body, and affirm that the mixture in the cup is His Blood?"

5:2:2
"If the body be not saved, then, in fact, neither did the Lord redeem us with His Blood; and neither is the cup of the Eucharist the partaking of His Blood nor is the Bread which we break the partaking of His Body ... He has declared the cup, a part of creation, to be His own Blood, from which He causes our blood to flow; and the bread, a part of creation, He has established as His own Body, from which gives increase to our bodies."

FATHERS OF THE THIRD CENTURY

Clement of Alexandria

(c. AD 150—inter 211/216)

Historical Note

Clement of Alexandria was born of pagan parents in Athens around the year AD 150. The circumstances concerning his conversion are unknown, but it is supposed that he was attracted to Christianity by the nobility and purity of its teachings. After his conversion, he traveled throughout southern Italy, Rome and then the Middle East seeking teachers to advance his Christian knowledge. In Alexandria, he met up with the celebrated Pantaenus and became a pupil in his school of catechumens (c. AD 180). Eventually, Clement was ordained a presbyter and rose to succeed Pantaenus around AD 200.

After only a brief number of years, Clement was forced to flee Egypt in the face of the persecution of Septimus Severus, making his way to Cappadocia. There, he met up with his former disciple, Bishop Alexander, and together they rendered faithful service to the people of the region. In AD 216, Bishop Alexander writes to Origen and speaks of Clement as having gone to his rest.

Clement possessed a broad and noble mind coupled with a sympathetic and noble character. He was very widely read and remembered much of what he encountered. No other ancient author knew or quoted as many pagan and Christian writers as he.

As a writer, Clement's chief aim was to determine the relationship between faith and reason and to show what philosophy had achieved as a preparation for the coming of Christian revelation. Philosophy is the tool by which the data given through Divine Revelation is to be transformed into a scientific theology.

Clement produced three great works:

(1) The *Exhortation to the Greeks (or Protreptikos)*. This is an apologetical work aimed at showing the influence of the Logos, or Divine Word, throughout history in the education of humanity. It is in twelve chapters and attacks the worthlessness and falsity of pagan beliefs and the inadequacy of philosophy without God and the true religion found in the teachings of the Prophets and Jesus Christ;
(2) *The Instructor of Children (or Paidagogos)* is a three-part sequel to the *Exhortation* and opens with an attack on the false knowledge of the Gnostics. True knowledge, rather, is a development of faith that begins with the illuminative effects of baptism. Clement then proceeds to present the Logos as an instructor of converts, particularly in regard to the conduct of Christians in a pagan world;
(3) The *Miscellanies (or Stromateis)* is a collection of eight books in which Clement treats a whole variety of different topics. These include the legitimacy of studying philosophy and the sciences, the relations between faith and Christian gnosis, marriage, martyrdom, and the religious life of a Christian, etc.

Other significant works of Clement include the *Hypotyposes*, an eight-volume commentary on the Old and New Testaments and the *Quis Dives Salvetur?*, a homily on Mark 10:17-31, filled with unction and pious reflections. Surviving fragments of other writings are mentioned by Eusebius.

Extracts

Exhortation to the Greeks (ante AD 200)

1:7:1
"This Word, then, the Christ, the cause of both our being at first (for He was in God) and of our well-being, this very Word has now appeared as

man, He alone being both, both God and man — the Author of all blessings to us; by whom we, being taught to live well, are sent on our way to life eternal. For, according to that inspired apostle of the Lord, the grace of God which bringeth salvation hath appeared to all men, teaching us, that, denying ungodliness and worldly lusts, we should live soberly, righteously, and godly, in this present world; looking for the blessed hope, and appearing of the glory of the great God and our Saviour Jesus Christ."

The Instructor of Children (ante AD 202)

1:6:26:1
"When we are baptized, we are enlightened. Being enlightened, we are adopted as sons. Adopted as sons, we are made perfect. Made perfect, we are become immortal. 'I say,' he declares, 'you are gods and sons of the Most High.' This work is variously called grace, illumination, perfection, and washing. It is a washing by which we are cleansed of sins; a gift of grace by which the punishments due our sins are remitted."

2:10
"Because of its divine institution for the propagation of man, the seed is not to be vainly ejaculated, nor is it to be damaged, nor is it to be wasted ... To have coitus other than to procreate children is to do injury to nature."

Miscellanies (post AD 202)

6:13:107:2
"Even here in the Church the gradations of bishops, presbyters, and deacons happen to be imitations, in my opinion, of the angelic glory and of that arrangement which, the Scriptures say, awaits those who have followed in the footsteps of the Apostles, and who have lived in perfect righteousness according to the Gospel."

6:14:108:4
"When we hear, 'Your faith has saved you,' we do not understand (The Lord) to say simply that they will be saved who have believed in whatever manner, even if works have not followed. To begin with, it was to the Jews

alone that He spoke this phrase, who had lived in accord with the law and blamelessly, and who had lacked only faith in the Lord."

6:17:157:4

"The thoughts of virtuous men are produced by divine inspiration. The soul is disposed in the way it is, and the will of God is conveyed to human souls, by special divine ministers who assist in such service. For regiments of angels are distributed over nations and cities; and perhaps some even are assigned to particular individuals."

7:12:70:4

"And one is not really shown to be a man in the choice of a single life; but he surpasses men, who, without pleasure or pain, has disciplined himself by marriage, by the begetting of children, and by care for the household; who, in his solicitude for the household, has been inseparable from God's love; and who has withstood every temptation arising through children and wife or through domestics and possessions. He, however, who is without a family, for the most part escapes temptation. Caring, then, for himself alone, he is surpassed by one who is inferior to him in what pertains to his own salvation, but is superior to him in the conduct of his life."

7:17:107:3

"From what has been said, then, it seems clear to me that the true Church, that which is really ancient, is one; and in it are enrolled those who, in accord with a design, are just ... We say, therefore, that in substance, in concept, in origin and in eminence, the ancient and Catholic Church is alone, gathering as it does into the unity of the one faith which results from the familiar covenants, – or rather, from the one covenant in different times, by the will of the one God and through the one Lord, – those already chosen, those predestined by God who knew before the foundation of the world that they would be just."

Fragments from *Clemens Alexandrinus* (Eusebius, *Ecclesiastical History* 6:14)

"Again, in the same books Clement has set down a tradition which he had received from the elders before him, in regard to the order of the Gospels, to the following effect. He says that the Gospels containing the genealogies were written first, and that the Gospel according to Mark was composed in the following circumstances: Peter having preached the word publicly at Rome, and by the Spirit proclaimed the Gospel, those who were present, who were numerous, entreated Mark, in as much as he had attended him from an early period, and remembered what had been said, to write down what had been spoken."

Tertullian

(inter AD 155/160–inter 240/250)

Historical Note

Tertullian's full name was Quintus Septimius Florens Tertullianus. He was born of pagan parents in Carthage just after the mid second century AD. His father was a Roman officer stationed in North Africa.

As a youth, Tertullian's life was not virtuous but it was laborious. He read intensely and studied whatever he could lay his hands upon. He became a lawyer of considerate repute, and after his conversion (c. AD 193) he employed his talents for the service and defense of Christianity. We do not know the circumstances of his conversion but we do know that it was sincere and thorough.

Tertullian was married and according to St Jerome was an ordained priest, though this is still in dispute as there is nothing in his writings to indicate this. Tixeront-Raemers (*Handbook of Patrology*, 1946, p. 110) dates his ordination towards the year AD 200. Nevertheless, his writings were widely known, read and quoted simply for their genuine excellence. He was the first great Latin Father and the pioneer of the African school that reached its climax in St Augustine.

Tertullian was a born fighter with an energetic mind and iron will. He fought continuously for what he believed to be right and good, waging incessant war against heresy and paganism. Unfortunately, he lacked moderation and tended to exaggeration, making Christian morality impracticable. His firmness often descended into stubbornness, a telltale sign of pride.

Tertullian's greatest works include the *Apology* and the *Demurrer Against the Heretics*. In the former he defends Christianity against the unjust legal measures taken against it and makes his famous declaration that "*The blood of the martyrs is the seed of the Church.*" In the latter he makes a general refutation of all dogmatic innovations through an affirmation of tradition and the authority of the Church.

Tertullian's writing career spanned the years AD 197-220. This span can be broken up into three distinct parts: his Catholic period AD 197-206; his semi-Montanist period AD 207-212; his Montanist period AD 213-220. The first period is marked by orthodoxy of opinion, the second by a rigorism and a developing anticlericalism without any definite break with the Catholic Church, the third by a clear defection to the Montanist camp.

The final break with Catholicism came with the formal condemnation of Montanism and Rome's authorization to contract second marriages after the death of the first spouse, a practice denounced by Montanists. Tertullian turned his apologetical pen against the Church, falling into an extreme anticlericalism and invective. After his defection, however, Tertullian's literary output declined markedly.

Some authors are of the view that Tertullian outgrew Montanism and founded his own sect which later became known as the Tertullianists. Records indicate that this sect subsisted until the end of the fourth century when St Augustine converted them. After AD 220, we do not hear of Tertullian. St Jerome remarks that he lived on into his eighties, possibly dying even as late as AD 250.

Extracts

Apology (AD 197)

9

"In our case, murder being once for all forbidden, we may not destroy even the foetus in the womb, while as yet the human being derives blood from other parts of the body for its sustenance. To hinder a birth is merely a speedier man killing; nor does it matter whether you take away a life that is born, or destroy one that is coming to the birth. That is a man which is going to be one."

21:6
"So also, that which proceeds from God is God and Son of God, and both are one. Likewise, as He is Spirit from Spirit, and God from God, He is made a second by count and in numerical sequence, but not in actual

condition; for He comes forth from the source but does not separate therefrom."

Demurrer Against the Heretics (AD 200)

19:3
"Wherever it shall be clear that the truth of the Christian discipline and faith are present, there also will be found the truth of the Scriptures and of their explanation, and of all the Christian traditions."

36:1
"How happy is that Church ... where Peter endured a passion like that of the Lord, where Paul was crowned in a death like John's."

28:1
"Grant, then, that all have erred; that the Apostle was mistaken in bearing witness; that the Holy Spirit had no such consideration for any one Church as to lead it into truth, although He was sent for that purpose by Christ, who had asked the Father to make Him the Teacher of truth; that the Steward of God and Vicar of Christ neglected His office, and permitted the Churches for a time to understand otherwise and to believe otherwise than He Himself had preached through the Apostles: now, is it likely that so many and such great Churches should have gone astray into a unity of faith?"

On Prayer (inter AD 200-206)

6:2
"This petition 'Give us today our daily bread' we understand rather in a spiritual sense, for Christ is our bread because he is life and bread of life. 'I am the bread of life,' he says, and, a little earlier, 'The bread is the word of the living God that has come down from heaven.' In addition, his body is a kind of bread: 'This is my body.' Consequently, in asking for daily bread, we are asking to live forever in Christ and never to be separated from his body."

To My Wife (inter AD 200-206)

2:8:6
"How shall we suffice for the telling of that happiness of that marriage which the Church arranges, which the sacrifice strengthens, on which the blessing sets a seal, which the angels proclaim, and which has the Father's approval?"

On Baptism (inter AD 200-206)

18:4
"According to circumstance and disposition and even age of the individual person, it may be better to delay Baptism; and especially so in the case of little children. Why, is it necessary - if it be not a case of necessity - that the sponsors too be thrust into danger, when they themselves may fail to fulfill their promises by reason of death, or ... be disappointed by the growth of an evil disposition?"

Against Marcion (inter AD 207-212)

1:18:2
"It is our definition that God must be known first from nature, and afterwards He is authenticated from instruction: by nature, from His works; by instruction, from His revelations."

The Soul (inter AD 208-212)

58:1
"In short, if we understand that prison of which the Gospel speaks to be Hades, and if we interpret the last farthing to be the light offense which is to be expiated there before the resurrection, no one will doubt that the soul undergoes some punishments in Hades, without prejudice to the fullness of the resurrection, after which recompense will be made through the flesh also."

Tertullian

The Resurrection of the Dead (inter AD 208-212)

8:3
"The flesh, then, is washed, so that the soul may be made clean. The flesh is anointed so that the soul may be dedicated to holiness. The flesh is signed, so that the soul too may be fortified. The flesh is shaded by the imposition of hands, so that the soul too may be illuminated by the Spirit. The flesh feeds on the Body and Blood of Christ, so that the soul may fatten on God."

The Flesh of Christ (c. AD 210)

17:5
"Likewise, through a Virgin, the Word of God was introduced to set up a structure of life. Thus, what had been laid waste in ruin by this sex, was by the same sex re-established in salvation. Eve had believed the serpent; Mary believed Gabriel. That which the one destroyed by believing, the other, by believing, set straight."

The Crown (AD 211)

3:3-5
"The Sacrament of the Eucharist, which the Lord commanded to be taken at meal times and by all, we take even before daybreak in congregations, but from the hand of none others except the presidents ... We offer sacrifices for the dead on their birthday anniversaries ... We take anxious care lest something of our Cup of Bread should fall upon the ground."

3:5
"At every forward step and movement, when coming in and going out, when putting on our clothes, when putting on our shoes, when bathing, when at table, when lighting the lamps, when reclining, when sitting, in all the ordinary occupations of our daily lives, we furrow our forehead with the sign."

Against Praxeas (post AD 213)

2:1

"We do indeed believe that there is only one God; but we believe that under this dispensation ... there is also a Son of this one only God, His Word, who proceeded from Him and through whom all things were made and without whom nothing was made. We believe that He was sent by the Father into a Virgin and was born of her, God and man, Son of man and Son of God, and was called by the name Jesus Christ. We believe that He suffered and that, in accord with the Scriptures, He died and was buried; and that He was raised again by the Father to resume His place in heaven, sitting at the right of the Father; and that He will come to judge the living and the dead. We believe that He sent down from the Father, in accord with His own promise, the Holy Spirit, the Paraclete, the Sanctifier of the faith of those who believe in the Father and in the Son and in the Holy Spirit ... That this rule of faith has been current since the beginning of the Gospel, before even the earlier heretics, - much more then, before Praxeas, who was but of yesterday."

St Hippolytus of Rome

(inter AD 170-175—235)

Historical Note

St Hippolytus was the first anti-pope and the only one honored as a saint. Not much is known of his early life besides the fact that there is evidence that he was of eastern origin, probably born in Alexandria between AD 170 and 175. This opinion rests on the fact that he was fluent in Greek and that his theological opinions reflect Alexandrian thought. He also says of himself that he was an intellectual disciple of St Irenaeus of Lyons. A tradition believed by St Jerome states that he was bishop of Porto Romanus, a nearby suburban Roman see.

By AD 212, St Hippolytus was establishing a reputation in Rome as a presbyter and scholar. Origen had the opportunity of hearing him while on a visit to Rome. St Hippolytus also worked side by side with Tertullian against the Gnostics and the Sabellians. During the reign of Pope Zephyrinus, St Hippolytus opposed his solution to the problem of Patripassianism, a solution devised with the help of his adviser St Callistus. When St Callistus was later elected Pope (AD 217-222), St Hippolytus opposed him openly for his alleged leniency towards repentant sinners, advocating a much more rigorous attitude. Gathering together a small group of devotees, St Hippolytus formed his own church and had himself elected as Bishop of Rome in opposition to St Callistus, thus effecting a formal schism.

This schism continued for eighteen years through the pontificates of St Urban I and St Pontian, ending in AD 235 with the outbreak of the Thracian persecution, which targeted leaders of the Church. In that year both Pope St Pontian and St Hippolytus were arrested and exiled by the Emperor Thrax to the unhealthy island of Sardinia. Together, they worked side by side in the salt mines. St Hippolytus witnessed firsthand the sanctity of Pope St Pontian and, humbled by the experience, he sent a message to his followers renouncing his claim to the See of Rome.

Soon after, both Pope St Pontian and St Hippolytus died in the salt mines. Since St Hippolytus had confessed his fault there was nothing to prevent his recognition as a true martyr. Pope St Fabian (AD 236–250) had his relics later brought back to Rome. A statue of St Hippolytus was discovered in 1551, apparently marking the site of his burial. His followers probably erected it shortly after his death.

St Hippolytus' writing activity was prodigious, but like Origen only a small percentage of it remains extant to this day. We possess only the titles of thirty-five of his works and even less texts. What we know comes mainly from the writings of Eusebius, St Jerome, Theodoret and Photius, This was probably due to the fact that he wrote in Greek at a time when Latin was fast becoming the official language of the Roman church, as well as the unhappy memory of his schism. He was undoubtedly a man of great talent with skills in exegesis, apology, dogma, morals, discipline, history and geography. Above all he was an exegete. As a preacher and homilist he exhibited true oratorical ability with a style that was clear, elegant and unaffected.

Extracts

Commentary on Daniel (c. AD 204)

1:16
"And she said to her maids, 'Bring me oil.' Indeed, faith and love prepare oil and cleansing unguents for those who are washed. But what were these unguents if not the commands of the Holy Word? And what the oil, if not the power of the Holy Spirit? It is with these, after the washing, that believers are anointed as with a sweet-smelling oil."

22
"For when the Gospel is preached in every place, the times being then accomplished ... the abomination of desolation will be manifested, and when he (the Antichrist) comes, the sacrifice and oblation will be removed, which are now offered up to God in every place by the gentiles."

23

"And then the deacons immediately bring the oblation to the bishop; and he eucharists the bread into the antitype of the Body of Christ; and the cup of mixed wine, for an antitype of the Blood, which was shed for all who believe in Him ... Indeed, the bishop shall explain the reason for all these things to those who partake. Breaking the Bread into individual particles which he then distributes, he shall say: 'Heavenly bread in Christ Jesus.' And he that receives shall answer: 'Amen.'"

The Apostolic Tradition (c. AD 215)

2

"Let the Bishop be ordained after he has been chosen by all the people. When someone pleasing to all has been named, let the people assemble on the Lord's Day with the presbyters and with such bishops as may be present. All giving assent, the bishops shall impose hands on him, and the presbytery shall stand by in silence. Indeed, all shall remain silent, praying in their hearts for the descent of the Spirit."

11

"When a widow is to be appointed, she is not to be ordained, but is designated by being named such ... A widow is appointed by words alone, and is then associated with the other widows. Hands are not imposed upon her, because she does not offer the oblation and she does not conduct the Liturgy. Ordination is for the clergy because of the Liturgy; but a widow is appointed for prayer, and prayer is the duty of all."

21

"Baptize first the children; and if they can speak for themselves, let them do so. Otherwise, let their parents or other relatives speak for them ... Do you believe in God, the Father almighty? Do you believe in Jesus Christ, the Son of God, who was born of the Virgin Mary by the Holy Spirit, has been crucified under Pontius Pilate, died [and was buried], who, on the third day rose again, alive, from the dead, ascended into heaven and took His seat at the right hand of the Father, and shall come to judge the living and the dead? Do you believe in the Holy Church and the resurrection of the body in the Holy Spirit?"

22

"The bishop, imposing his hands on them, shall make an invocation saying: 'O Lord God, who made them worthy of the remission of sins through the Holy Spirit's washing unto rebirth, send into them your grace so that they may serve you according to your will: for there is glory to you, to the Father and the Son with the Holy Spirit, in the Holy Church, both now and through the ages of ages, Amen.' Then, pouring the consecrated oil into his hands and imposing it on the head of the baptized, he shall say: 'I anoint you with holy oil in the Lord, the Father Almighty and Christ Jesus and the Holy Spirit.' And signing them on the forehead he shall kiss them and say: 'The Lord shall be with you.' And he that has been signed shall say: 'And with your spirit.' Thus shall he do with each."

Refutation of All Heresies (post AD 222)

9:12

"For this reason women who were reputed to be believers began to take drugs to render themselves sterile, and being conceived, since they would not, on account of relatives and excessive wealth, want to have a child by a slave or by any insignificant person. See, then, into what great impiety that lawless one has proceeded, by teaching adultery and murder at the same time."

9:12

"For Christ is the God over all, who has arranged to wash away sin from mankind, rendering the old man new."

Against the Greeks (ante AD 225)

3

"Standing before (Christ's) judgment, all of them, men, angels, and demons, crying out in one voice, shall say: 'Just is your judgment!' And the justice of that cry will be apparent in the recompense made to each. To those who have done well, everlasting enjoyment shall be given; while to the lovers of evil shall be given eternal punishment."

Origen

(c. AD 185–253/254)

Historical Note

Origen was born around the year AD 185 of Christian parents in Alexandria. His father, St Leonidas, was martyred in AD 202 during the reign of Septimus Severus. In his teenage years Origen became a disciple of Pantaenus and Clement and showed very early on that he possessed a mind of insatiable curiosity and diligence.

Though only eighteen years of age and a layman, Origen was given control of the catechetical school of Alexandria by Bishop Demetrius after the exile of Clement. Between AD 204 and 230, Origen raised it to its greatest prominence. While teaching, though, he was still studying and acquired knowledge of Neo-Platonism and Hebrew. He grasped all the Scriptural, theological and philosophical reasoning of his time.

Origen was the most prodigious writer of all time. He was above all a Scripture scholar and formulated almost his entire theology in his written commentaries on the Sacred texts. A wealthy pupil of his, Ambrosius, placed at Origen's disposal an abundance of secretaries and copyists. St Jerome and Eusebius knew of some two thousand works produced by Origen. St Epiphanius gives the figure as six thousand. Such prodigiousness earned Origen the title of greatest scholar of Christian antiquity.

The major works of Origen can be briefly listed as follows:

1. *The Hexalpa*: This work contained six different Hebrew and Greek versions of the Old Testament in six parallel columns to compare and contrast them so to detect at a glance the true meaning of a passage;
2. *The Scholia*: Briefs notes on the more difficult passages of Scripture;
3. *The Homilies*: Familiar talks with the faithful on the Scriptures;
4. *The Commentaries*: Written works to explain the texts of the Scriptures in a scientific way to his readers;

5. *Against Celsus*: An apologetical work against the Platonist Celsus who had launched a learned and caustic attack against Christianity;
6. *Fundamental Doctrines*: An early Summa Theologica in four volumes aimed at bringing together the fundamental teachings of Christianity and treating them in a systematic way.

Due to the persecution of Emperor Caracalla in AD 215, Origen left Alexandria and made his way to Caesarea in Palestine. There, Bishops Theoctistus and Alexander allowed him to preach to the congregation on Scripture, to the ire of Bishop Demetrius of Alexandria who demanded Origen's return to Egypt.

Fifteen years later, Origen again passed through Caesarea, and in order to pre-empt any objections to his preaching, Bishops Theoctistus and Alexander ordained him to the priesthood. This was in violation of the canons and thoroughly enraged Bishop Demetrius, who then convoked two synods in Alexandria in AD 230 and 231 which deposed, degraded and excommunicated Origen. Bishop Demetrius then sent special letters to all the other major churches notifying them of the measures taken.

Banished from Alexandria, Origen then moved to Caesarea where he founded a school in the style of that of Alexandria for over twenty years. One of his famous pupils there was St Gregory Thaumaturgus. Origen survived the persecution of Emperor Thrax (AD 235-237) but during the Decian persecution he was arrested, imprisoned and tortured, dying as a result of his sufferings in Tyre in AD 253 or 254 at the age of 69.

During his lifetime, Origen was never suspected of heresy. He was always acknowledged as a great scholar and theologian who endeavored to be faithful to Catholic teaching. The controversies that arose over his writings occurred on three separate occasions at the beginning of the fourth, fifth and sixth centuries. Origen was subsequently declared to have taught error and certain propositions of his declared formally heretical. This accounts for the large-scale destruction and loss of many of his writings, as well as many other expurgations, interpolations and retranslations. We now possess a little more than one-hundredth of what he produced, and this of poor quality and preservation.

Extracts

Fundamental Doctrines (c. AD 220)

1:Preface:2
"Although there are many who believe that they themselves hold to the teachings of Christ, there are yet some among them who think differently from their predecessors. The teaching of the Church has indeed been handed down through an order of succession from the Apostles, and remains in the Churches even to the present time. That alone is to be believed as the truth which is in no way at variance with ecclesiastical and apostolic tradition."

On Prayer (post AD 231)

11:2
"Now the one great virtue according to the Word of God is love of one's neighbor. We must believe that the saints who have died possess this love in a far higher degree towards the ones engaged in the combat of life than those who are still subject to human weakness and involved in the combat along with their weaker brethren. The words 'If one member suffer anything, all the members suffer with it, or if one member glory, all the members rejoice with it' are not confined to those on earth who love their brethren. For the words apply just as much to the love of those who have left this present life ...'

Commentaries on St John (inter AD 226-232)

19:6
"Whoever dies in his sins, even if he profess to believe in Christ, does not truly believe in Him; and even if that which exists without works be called faith, such faith is dead in itself, as we read in the Epistle bearing the name of James."

Homilies on Luke (post AD 233)

Hom. 12
"To every man there are two attending angels, the one of justice and the other of wickedness. If there be good thoughts in our heart, and if righteousness be welling up in our soul, it can scarcely be doubted that an angel of the Lord is speaking to us. If, however, the thoughts of our heart be turned to evil, an angel of the Devil is speaking to us."

Commentaries on Romans (post AD 244)

5:8
"Why, when the Lord Himself told His disciples that they should baptize all peoples in the name of the Father and of the Son and of the Holy Spirit, does this Apostle employ the name of Christ alone in Baptism, saying, 'we who have been baptized in Christ'; for indeed, legitimate Baptism is had only in the name of the Trinity."

Homilies on Numbers (post AD 244)

Hom. 7:2
"Formally, in an obscure way, there was manna for food; now, however, in full view, there is the true food, the flesh of the word of God, as He Himself says: 'My flesh is truly food, and My Blood is truly drink.'"

Homilies on Leviticus (post AD 244)

Hom. 2:4
"In addition to these there is also a seventh, albeit hard and laborious: the remission of sins through penance, when the sinner washes his pillow with tears, when his tears are day and night his nourishment, and when he does not shrink from declaring his sin to a priest of the Lord and from seeking medicine, after the manner of him who says, 'I said, to the Lord I will accuse myself of my iniquity, and you forgave the disloyalty of my heart.'"

Commentaries on Matthew (post AD 244)

14:16
"Certainly it is God who joins two in one, so that when He marries a woman to a man, there are no longer two. And since it is God who joins them, there is in this joining a grace for those who are joined by God. Paul knew this, and he said that just as holy celibacy was a grace so also was marriage according to the word of God a grace. He says, 'I would that all men were like myself; but each has his own grace from God, one in this way, another in that.'"

Homilies on Leviticus (post AD 244)

Hom. 8:3
"According to the usage of the Church, Baptism is given even to infants. And indeed if there were nothing in infants which required a remission of sins and nothing in them pertinent to forgiveness, the grace of Baptism would seem superfluous."

St Cyprian of Carthage

(inter AD 200-210—258)

Historical Note

St Cyprian's full name was Caecilius Cyprianus Thascius. He was born into a wealthy pagan family in Carthage somewhere between the years AD 200 and 210. As a young man he had a thorough education, later embarking on a career as a rhetorician and also practised law. In these professions he soon assumed some prominence and became acquainted with the most distinguished individuals of Carthage.

However, St Cyprian was plagued by many vices and lived a life of indulgence. About AD 245 he met the venerable priest Caecilianus and soon after converted to Christianity. St Cyprian's conversion was complete and is beautifully described in his letter to his friend Donatus: "*I indulged my sins as if they were actually part and parcel of myself. But afterwards, when the stain of my past life had been washed away by means of the water of re-birth, a light from above poured itself upon my chastened and now pure heart*" (Ad Donatus 4). Soon after, St Cyprian was ordained to the priesthood and then to the episcopate (c. AD 248-249).

St Cyprian was an assiduous reader of the works of Tertullian and often referred to him as "The Teacher." However, unlike Tertullian, St Cyprian was patient and well-balanced, commanding respect through his dignified aspect, while his simplicity, charity and cordiality endeared him to all that knew him. His numerous letters and thirteen works (dealing with apologetics, morals or ecclesiastical discipline) reflect his calm and equable temperament. He was a man of authority and through his personal influence made his See the center of the whole African church (Tixeront-Raemers, *Handbook of Patrology* 1943, pp. 120-121).

St Cyprian's episcopate lasted only nine years but it was full of events and activity. As bishop of Carthage, he directed the affairs of his flock during the persecution of the Emperor Decius (AD 250). From a prudently chosen safe haven in the hills outside Carthage he composed numerous letters exhorting his clergy to maintain their perseverance and that of the faithful throughout the time of trial.

St Cyprian returned to Carthage in the spring of AD 251 and was immediately confronted with the question of the *Lapsi*. During the persecution, many of the faithful apostatized, only to seek reconciliation after the storm had passed. This posed a problem for St Cyprian who did not favor their easy reconciliation. Factionalism ensued and one priest, Novatus, broke ranks with St Cyprian and made his way to Rome where, ironically, he joined the heresy of Novatian who generally opposed reconciliation of the lapsed entirely. A balanced imposition of moderate penance by St Cyprian brought the issue of the *Lapsi* to a successful conclusion.

Of even greater significance was the dispute between St Cyprian and Pope St Stephen I (AD 254-256) concerning the baptism of heretics. It had been the immemorial custom of the Church in Africa to reject the baptism of heretics as invalid and St Cyprian maintained this attitude. Pope St Stephen I sharply contested this and issued severe warnings against St Cyprian. However, St Cyprian refused to yield and the dispute dangerously had the potential to erupt into open schism between Rome and Africa. Schism was only avoided with the outbreak of another Roman persecution initiated by the Emperor Valerian. Due to his persecutory decree, both Pope St Stephen I and St Cyprian were arrested and martyred. St Cyprian, after a year of exile in Curubis was summoned to offer sacrifice to the gods. Upon his refusal, he was beheaded outside Carthage on 14 September, AD 258. The records of his martyrdom are still extant and provide wonderful reading.

Extracts

Letter to His Clergy and to All His People (AD 250)

39 (34):3

"Lawrence and Ignatius, though they fought betimes in worldly camps, were true and spiritual soldiers of God; and while they laid the Devil on his back with their confession of Christ, they merited the palms and crowns of the Lord by their illustrious passion. We always offer sacrifices for them, as you will recall, as often as we celebrate the passions of the martyrs by commemorating their anniversary day."

The Lapsed (AD 251)

17
"The Lord alone is able to have mercy. He alone, who bore our sins, who grieved for us, and whom God delivered up for our sins, is able to grant pardon for the sins which have been committed against Him ... Certainly we believe that the merits of the martyrs and the works of the just will be of great avail with the Judge - but that will be when the day of judgment comes, when, after the end of this age and of the world, His people shall stand before the tribunal of Christ."

29
"I beseech you, brethren, let everyone who has sinned confess his sin while he is still in this world, while his confession is still admissible, while satisfaction and remission made through the priests are pleasing before the Lord."

Letter to all His People (AD 251)

43 (40):5
"There is one God and one Christ, and one Church, and one Chair founded on Peter by the word of the Lord. It is not possible to set up another altar or for there to be another priesthood besides that one altar and that one priesthood. Whoever has gathered elsewhere is scattering."

The Lord's Prayer (c. AD 251-252)

18
"As the prayer continues, we ask and say, 'Give us this day our daily bread' ... And we ask that this bread be given to us daily, so that we who are in Christ and daily receive the Eucharist as the food of salvation, may not, by falling into some more grievous sin and then in abstaining from communicating, be withheld from the heavenly Bread, and be separated from Christ's Body ... He Himself warns us, saying, 'Unless you eat the

flesh of the Son of Man and drink His blood, you shall not have life in you.' Therefore do we ask that our Bread, which is Christ, be given to us daily, so that we who abide and live in Christ may not withdraw from His sanctification and from His Body."

Letters to Fidus (c. AD 251-252)

64 (59):5

"As to what pertains to the case of infants: you said that they ought not to be baptized within the second or third day after their birth ... and that you did not think that one should be baptized and sanctified within the eighth day after his birth. In our council it seemed to us far otherwise."

Letter to Cornelius of Rome (c. AD 252)

59 (55):14

"With a false bishop appointed for themselves by heretics, they dare even to set sail and carry letters from schismatics and blasphemers to the chair of Peter and to the principal Church, in which sacerdotal unity has its source; nor did they take thought that these are Romans, whose faith was praised by the preaching Apostle, and among whom it is not possible for perfidy to have entrance."

Letter to the People of Thibar (AD 253)

58:10

"Oh, what a day that will be, and how great when it comes, dearest brethren! when the Lord begins to survey His people and to recognize by examining with divine knowledge the merits of each individual! to cast into hell evildoers, and to condemn our persecutors to the eternal fire and punishing flame! and indeed, to present to us the reward of faith and devotion! What will be that glory, and how great the joy of being admitted to the sight of God! to be so honored as to receive the joy of eternal light and salvation in the presence of Christ the Lord, your God!"

Epistle to Caecilius on the Sacrament of the Cup of the Lord (AD 253)

4
"In the priest Melchizedek we see prefigured the sacrament of the sacrifice of the Lord, according to what divine Scripture testifies, 'And Melchizedek, king of Salem, brought forth bread and wine' ... For who is more a priest of the most high God than Our Lord Jesus Christ, who offered a sacrifice to God the Father, and offered that very same thing which Melchizedek had offered, that is, bread and wine, to wit, His body and blood? ... In Genesis therefore, that the benediction ... might be duly celebrated, the figure of Christ's sacrifice precedes as ordained in bread and wine; which thing the Lord, completing and fulfilling, offered bread and the cup mixed with wine, and so He who is the fullness of truth fulfilled the truth of the image prefigured."

Letter to Florentius Pupianus (AD 254)

66 (69):8
"There speaks Peter, upon whom the Church would be built, teaching in the name of the Church and showing that even if a stubborn and proud multitude withdraws because it does not wish to obey, yet the Church does not withdraw from Christ. The people joined to the priest and the flock clinging to their shepherd are the Church."

Letter to Jubaianus (c. AD 254-256)

73:9
"For the reason, then, that they had already received legitimate and ecclesiastical Baptism, it was not necessary to baptize them again. Rather, that only which was lacking was done by Peter and John; and thus, prayer having been made over them, and hands having been imposed upon them, the Holy Spirit was invoked and was poured out upon them. This is even now the practice among us, so that those who are baptized in the Church are then brought to the prelates of the Church; and through our prayer and the imposition of hands, they receive the Holy Spirit and are perfected with the seal of the Lord."

Lactantius

(inter AD 240-250—post 317)

Historical Note

Lactantius' full name was Lucius Caelius Firmianus Lactantius. Born between the years AD 240 and 250 in Numidia, Africa, he studied under Arnobius and became a master rhetorician by profession. He worked with significant success in Africa before being summoned around the year AD 290 by the Emperor Diocletian to teach rhetoric in his capital Nicomedia.

However, having little work to do in a Greek-speaking city the Latin-speaking Lactantius turned to writing books. By AD 303, he had converted to Christianity. As a consequence, he was obliged to resign from his teaching position due to the recent imperial decree of Diocletian (Feb. 24) forbidding Christians from holding public offices.

In AD 305, Lactantius left Bithynia and lived a life of obscurity and poverty, passing through the persecutions untouched until recalled by the Emperor Constantine around AD 317 to tutor his son Crispus in Latin. It was during the intervening years that Lactantius composed his most important work *The Divine Institutions*, a seven-volume refutation of paganism and defense of Christianity in a form pleasing to cultured minds. Book I deals with the unity of God and refutes polytheism; Book II demonstrates that paganism cannot be true worship; Book III shows that philosophy by itself cannot give man all the truth he needs; Books IV-VII expounds the truth of Christianity, its moral and discipline systems and its beliefs about the end of the world and everlasting life. Despite its doctrinal shortcomings and theological mediocrity, it is the first valuable Latin summary of the Christian faith.

Lactantius was a sincere Christian who possessed a peaceful and well-balanced disposition. He did his work quietly without seeking attention. As a writer his works exhibit order, measure and harmony. What remains of his writings include four apologetical, one historical and one poetical work. His *Deaths of the Persecutors* is a remarkably accurate history of the persecutions from Nero to Diocletian and points to the miserable deaths of the tyrannical Emperors as a just chastisement for their cruelties. Lactantius died soon after AD 317, the exact time and place being unknown.

Extracts

The Divine Institutions (inter AD 304-310)

4:13:1
"He was made both Son of God in the spirit and Son of man in the flesh: that is, both God and man."

4:29:3
"When we speak of God the Father and of God the Son, we do not speak of them as diverse, nor do we separate them from each other; for without the Son the Father cannot be; nor separated from the Father, can the Son be. Indeed, without the Son, the Father cannot be so named, nor can the Son be generated without the Father ... both have one mind, one spirit, one substance."

4:30:11
"It is therefore, the Catholic Church alone which retains true worship. This is the fountain of truth; this, the domicile of faith; this, the temple of God. Whoever does not enter there or whoever does not go out from here, he is a stranger to the hope of life and salvation ... Because, however, all the various groups of heretics are confident that they are the Christians, and think that theirs is the Catholic Church, let it be known: that is the true Church, in which there is confession and penance, and which takes a salubrious care of the sins and wounds to which the weak flesh is subject."

6:23:33
"Lest anyone think that he can circumvent the divine commands, these points are added in order to remove all occasion of chicanery or deceit: he is an adulterer, who married a woman divorced from her husband, or who divorced a wife on account of any crime except adultery, so that he might

marry another; for God did not wish the body to be broken and torn apart."

7:21:3
"The Holy writings teach us, however, that the impious are to be given punishments. Because they committed sins in their bodies, they will again be clothed with flesh, so that in their bodies they can make expiation. Yet, it will not be that flesh which God put upon man. It will be similar to the earthly flesh, but indestructible and lasting forever, so that it will be able to hold together under torture and under eternal fire, the nature of which is different from the common fire we use for the necessities of life, and which is extinguished unless it is nourished by fuel of some material kind."

18 (?)
"For if homicide is wicked because it is a destroyer of a man, he who kills himself is fettered by the same guilt because he kills a man. In fact, this ought to be judged a greater crime, the punishment of which belongs to God alone. For, just as we came into this life not of our own accord, so departure from this domicile of the body which was a sign to our protection must be made at the order of the same One who put us into this body, to dwell therein until He should order us to leave."

The Deaths of the Persecutors (inter AD 316-320)

2:5
"When Nero was already reigning Peter came to Rome, where, in virtue of the performance of certain miracles which he worked by that power of God which had been given to him, he converted many to righteousness and established a firm and steadfast temple to God. When this fact was reported to Nero, he noticed that not only at Rome but everywhere great multitudes were daily abandoning the worship of idols, and, condemning their old ways, were going over to the new religion. Being that he was a detestable and pernicious tyrant, he sprang to the task of tearing down the heavenly temple and destroying righteousness. It was he that first persecuted the servants of God. Peter, he fixed to a cross; and Paul, he slew."

NICENE AND POST NICENE FATHERS

St Athanasius of Alexandria

(c. AD 295–373)

Historical Note

St Athanasius was born about AD 295 near the city of Alexandria. His parents were pagans but St Athanasius converted at an early age. He grew up during the last of the official Roman imperial persecutions and witnessed the triumph of Constantine that resulted in the liberty of the Church. However, peace would be short-lived with the rise of Arianism and its denials of the divinity of Christ. The Arian whirlwind caught all virtually by surprise. As St Jerome declared, "I awoke and found the world Arian." Up to ninety-eight percent of the Bishops in the East succumbed to Arianism. The number of Bishops that resisted was literally only a handful.

With Arianism causing contention and strife throughout the Empire, the Emperor Constantine agreed to resolve the crisis by summoning a general council of Bishops to meet at Nicaea commencing 20 May, AD 325. St Athanasius accompanied the great bishop St Alexander of Alexandria to the Council as his deacon and secretary. St Alexander had already proven himself to be an implacable enemy of Arius by formally condemning him as a heretic in two encyclical letters written c. AD 322.

At the Council, St Athanasius shone as the champion of orthodoxy, convincing the Council Fathers to condemn Arianism and proclaim Christ as *homo-ousious*, that is, "as the same substance" as the

Father. From the Council issued the great *Nicene Creed*, which remains the symbol of orthodox faith to this day.

Though condemned, Arianism would linger on for centuries to come. Arius himself would die an impious death in AD 336, while St Athanasius succeeded St Alexander on 8 June, AD 328. St Athanasius' career as bishop of Alexandria was an extremely stormy one. Due to his staunch defence of the Nicene teaching he was exiled five times from his see (in AD 335, 340, 356, 362, 365), incurring the wrath of Emperors Constantine, Constantius, Julian the Apostate and Valens in the process. All up, St Athanasius spent more than one-third of his episcopate away from his see. He was attacked, calumnied, formally condemned and pursued. He survived partly due to his determined, inflexible and noble character and supreme confidence that sooner or later God would make truth prevail. He never wavered or compromised even during the darkest hours. He was a true leader whose authority and counsel were never questioned. Only in his last seven years from AD 366 to 373 did St Athanasius remain undisturbed.

As a writer, St Athanasius was not refined, nor did he possess a great knowledge of the classics. Yet he had a clear mind and composed with firmness and logic. He knew what to say and put his whole soul into saying it. He never wrote just for the sake of writing, but did so to plead the cause of the Nicene faith and confound his opponents. In his works can be distinguished the exegetical, apologetical, dogmatic, polemical, moral, disciplinary and the epistol.

Extracts

Treatise on the Incarnation of the Word (c. AD 318)

8:3
"If the Son of God had wanted merely to appear, he could certainly have assumed any kind of body, even one better than ours. Instead it was our own kind of body that he took, and not just in any way. He took it from a pure and unstained Virgin, who had not known man."

47:2
"And while in times past demons, occupying springs or rivers or trees or

stones, cheated men by deceptive appearances and imposed upon the credulous by their juggleries, now, after the divine coming of the Word, an end is put to their deceptions. For by the sign of the cross, a man but using it, their wiles are put to flight."

Apology Against the Arians (c. AD 347)

3:29

"It was for our sake that Christ became man, taking flesh from the Virgin Mary, Mother of God."

Letter Concerning the Decrees of the Council of Nicaea (c. AD 350-351)

20

"The generation of the Son from the Father is otherwise than that which accords with the nature of men; and he is not only like, but is in fact inseparable from the substance of the Father. He and the Father are indeed one, as he did say himself; and the Word is ever in the Father and the Father in the Word, as is the way of radiance in relation to light. The term itself indicates this; and the Council, so understanding the matter, did well, therefore, when it wrote homoousios, so that it might defeat the perverseness of the heretics, while proclaiming that the Word is other than created things."

27

"And concerning the everlasting co-existence of the Word with the Father, and that He is not of another essence or subsistence, but proper to the Father's, as the Bishops in the Council said, you may hear again from the labor-loving Origen also ... 'But it is not innocent nor without peril, if because of our weakness of understanding we deprive God, as far as in us lies, of the Only-begotten Word ever co-existing with Him; and the Wisdom in which He rejoiced; else He must be conceived as not always possessed of joy.' See, we are proving that this view has been transmitted from father to father; but ye, O modern Jews and disciples of Caiaphas, how many fathers can ye assign to your phrases?"

The Monk's History of the Arian Impiety (AD 358)

52

"For if a judgment had been passed by Bishops, what concern had the Emperor with it? Or if it was only a threat of the Emperor, what need in that case was there of the so-named Bishops? When was such a thing heard of before from the beginning of the world? When did a judgement of the Church receive its validity from the Emperor? or rather when was his decree ever recognised by the Church? There have been many Councils held heretofore; and many judgements passed by the Church; but the Fathers never sought the consent of the Emperor thereto, nor did the Emperor busy himself with the affairs of the Church."

Four Letters to Serapion of Thmuis (c. AD 359-360)

1:24

"We are all said to be partakers of God through the Holy Spirit. 'Do you not know,' it says, 'that you are a temple of God, and the Spirit of God dwells in you? If anyone ruins the temple of God, him will God ruin; for it is holy, this temple of God, which is just what you are.' If the Holy Spirit were a creature, there could be no communion of God with us through him. On the contrary, we would be joined to a creature, and we would be foreign to the divine nature, as having nothing in common with it ... But if by participation in the Spirit we are made partakers in the divine nature, it is insanity for anyone to say that the Spirit has a created nature and not the nature of God."

Letter on the Councils of Rimini and Seleucia (AD 361-362)

5

"Without prefixing Consulate, month, and day, (the Fathers) wrote concerning Easter, 'It seemed good as follows,' for it did then seem good that there should be a general compliance; but about the faith they wrote not, 'It seemed good,' but, 'thus believes the Catholic Church'; and thereupon they confessed how they believed, in order to show that their own sentiments were not novel, but Apostolic; and what they wrote down was no discovery of theirs, but is the same as was taught by the Apostles."

On the Incarnation of the Word of God Against the Arians (c. AD 365)

21

"And when (Christ) says, 'Father, if it be possible, let this chalice pass from me; yet, not my will be done, but yours'; and 'the spirit is ready, but the flesh is weak,' He gives evidence therein of two wills, the one human, which is of the flesh, and the one divine, which is of God. That which is human, because of the weakness of the flesh, shrinks from suffering. That, however, which is divine, is ready."

Festal Letter 39 (AD 367)

7

"But for greater exactness I add this also, writing of necessity; that there are other books besides these not indeed included in the Canon, but appointed by the Fathers to be read by those who newly join us, and who wish for instruction in the word of godliness. The Wisdom of Solomon, and the Wisdom of Sirach, and Esther, and Judith, and Tobit, and that which is called the Teaching of the Apostles, and the Shepherd. But the former, my brethren, are included in the Canon, the latter being [merely] read; nor is there in any place a mention of apocryphal writings. But they are an invention of heretics, who write them when they choose, bestowing upon them their approbation, and assigning to them a date, that so, using them as ancient writings, they may find occasion to lead astray the simple."

Sermon to the Newly Baptized (ante AD 373)
[Quoted by St Eutyches, Patriarch of Constantinople (+ AD 582) in his *Sermo de Paschate et de Sacrosancta Eucharistia*]
"Let us approach the celebration of the mysteries. This bread and this wine, so as long as the prayers and supplications have not taken place, remain simply what they are. But after the great prayers and holy supplications have been sent forth, the Word comes down into the bread and wine - and thus is his Body confected."

De Virginitate, in *Le Museon* (1958)

42:243-244
"But since she was a virgin, and was his Mother, he gave her as a mother to his disciple, even though she was not really John's mother, because of his great purity of understanding and because of her untouched virginity."

Homily of the Papyrus of Turin, in *Le Museon* (1958)

71:216
"O noble Virgin, truly you are greater than any other greatness. For who is your equal in greatness, O dwelling place of God the Word? To whom among all creatures shall I compare you, O Virgin? You are greater than them all O Covenant, clothed with purity instead of gold! You are the Ark in which is found the golden vessel containing the true manna, that is, the flesh in which divinity resides."

Eusebius Pamphilus

(c. AD 263–340)

Historical Note

Eusebius, the great Father of Church history, was born in Caesarea, Palestine, around AD 263. In his early years, Eusebius studied under the presbyters Dorotheus and Pamphilus, the latter being the distinguished successor to Origen's school in Caesarea. It was out of respect for this teacher that Eusebius took the name of Pamphilus. It was also in Caesarea that Eusebius received some of the misleading phrases on the Word that would lead him later into Semi-Arianism.

Eusebius was ordained to the priesthood by Bishop Agapius and worked with Pamphilus to enrich the library of Caesarea with new manuscripts. His gentle, agreeable and irenic character suited him for this work and his studies in the future. He survived the Diocletian persecution; however, Pamphilus was not so fortunate.

In AD 313, Eusebius was appointed to the see of Caesarea. There then followed a period of peace lasting over ten years. It was during this period that Eusebius began writing his most reputable works.

Soon after, he became directly embroiled in the Arian controversy. Despite signing the Nicene Creed (due to pressure from the Emperor Constantine), Eusebius adopted openly a middle semi-Arian position for the sake of compromise and peace within the Church. This position, known specifically as *Homoianism*, accepted the likeness of the Father and the Son without reference to their substance. He also publicly defended his namesake, the Arian Eusebius of Nicomedia, and took part in the Council of Antioch in AD 330 which deposed Eustathius, and the Council of Tyre in AD 335 which excommunicated, deposed and sent St Athanasius into exile. Eusebius may have opposed St Athanasius and his followers also because of their zeal, which he saw as disturbing the peace of the Church.

Eusebius was very close to the Emperor Constantine and had his ear at all times. He also tended to flatter Constantine and was servile to his demands. For this he was criticized in his time and by later Church historians as being the prototype of weak-kneed court bishops who fail to stand up to civil rulers infected by Caesero-papism.

Eusebius' greatest work is his *Ecclesiastical History*, written between AD 300 and 325. It is an apologetical history aimed at proving the truth of Christianity. The original Greek version in several manuscripts is still extant, together with a Latin (unfaithful) translation by Rufinus of Aquileia updated to AD 395. Eusebius' other works comprise books on history, apologetics, Scripture, dogma, discourses and letters. They include, namely, *Life of Pamphilus, Martyr*; *On the Martyrs of Palestine*; *Acts of Ancient Martyrs*; *The Chronicle*; *Life of Constantine*. Though regarded as a great scholar, very few of his works entitle him to be regarded as a theologian of significance. Eusebius remained actively writing until the end of his life, which took place no later than AD 340.

Extracts

The Chronicle (c. AD 303)

Ad An. Dom. 42
"The second year of the two hundredth and fifth Olympiad the apostle Peter, after he has established the Church in Antioch, is sent to Rome, where he remains a bishop of that city, preaching the gospel for twenty five years ..."

Ad An. Dom. 43
"Third year of the two hundredth and fifth olympiad: the Evangelist Mark, interpreter of Peter, announces Christ in Egypt and Alexandria."

Ad An. Dom. 68
"Nero is the first, in addition to all other crimes, to make a persecution against the Christians, in which Peter and Paul died gloriously in Rome."

Ecclesiastical History (inter AD 303-325)

2:14: 6
"In the same reign of Claudius, the all-good and gracious providence which watches over all things guided Peter, the great and mighty among the Apostles, who, because of his virtue, was the spokesman for all the others, to Rome."

2:15:4
"It is said that Peter's first epistle, in which he makes mention of Mark, was composed at Rome itself; and that he himself indicates this, referring to the city figuratively as Babylon, in these words: 'She that is the elect in Babylon greets you, as does also my son Mark.' They say that this Mark was the first to be sent to preach in Egypt the Gospel which, indeed, he had written, and that he was the first to establish churches in Alexandria itself."

2:25:8 [Fragment in Eusebius: Dionysius of Corinth, *To Pope Soter* (c. AD 170)]
"You have also, by your very admonition, brought together the planting that was made by Peter and Paul at Rome and at Corinth; for both of them alike planted in our Corinth and taught us; and both alike, teaching similarly in Italy, suffered martyrdom at the same time."

3:1:1
"The holy Apostles and disciples of the Savior, however, were scattered throughout the whole world. Thomas, as tradition holds, received Parthia by lot; Andrew, Scythia; John, Asia, busying himself among the people there until he died at Ephesus. Peter, however, seems to have preached to the Jews in the diaspora in the Pontus and in Galatia, Bithynia, Cappadocia, and in Asia; and at last, having come to Rome, he was crucified head downwards, the manner in which he himself had thought it fitting to suffer. Is it needful to say anything of Paul, who fulfilled the gospel of Christ from Jerusalem to Illyricum, and afterwards in the time of Nero was martyred in Rome?"

3:3:1

"So much, then, for the works attributed to Peter, of which I recognize only one Epistle as genuine and agreed upon by the ancient presbyters. The fourteen of Paul are obvious and certain; but wait, it is not right to ignore that some have disputed the Epistle to the Hebrews, saying that it was rejected by the Church of Rome as not being by Paul."

3:25:1

"Among the disputed books, which are nevertheless known to most, there are extant the Epistles said to be of James, and of Jude, and the second of Peter; and the second and third attributed to John, whether they happen to be by the Evangelist, or by someone else having that same name. Among the spurious writings must be reckoned the Acts of Paul, the writing called The Shepherd, the Apocalypse of Peter, and in addition to these, the Epistle attributed to Barnabas, and the so-called Teachings of the Apostles; and too, as I said, the Apocalypse of John, if it so be judged. For, as I said, some reject it, while others include it among the recognized books."

Preparation for the Gospel (inter AD 314-320)

1:4

"Persians, when they have become pupils of the Savior, no longer marry their own mothers. Neither do the Scythians, since the word of Christ has penetrated their lands, any longer feed on human flesh. Other tribes of barbarians no longer have unlawful relations with their daughters and sisters; nor do men fall madly in love with men and indulge those pleasures which are contrary to nature."

Proof of the Gospel (inter AD 316-322)

1:10

"... when we have a daily celebrating of the memory of His Body and of His Blood, regarded as worthy of worship and as a sacrifice more sublime than those of antiquity, then certainly we no longer think that it could be in accord with the dictates of religion to fall back into those first and weak foreshadowings, which are symbols and images but which do not embrace the same truth."

Didymus the Blind

(c. AD 313–398)

Historical Note

Didymus was born in Alexandria around AD 313. Although becoming blind at the age of four, he never prayed for the return of his sight but for illumination of the heart. Didymus developed an insatiable desire for knowledge and through an indomitable will became one of the most learned men of his time.

Appointed head of the catechetical school of Alexandria by St Athanasius, Didymus had as his more famous students and hearers St Antony of the Desert, Palladius, Evargrius Ponticus, St Jerome and Rufinus of Aquilaea. St Jerome often spoke of Didymus not as the blind but as "the Seer." Didymus remained head of the catechetical school for over half a century.

Probably as a consequence of his blindness, Didymus was able to develop a prolific memory and gained a vast knowledge of philosophy and theology as well as other secular sciences. He was also noted for his exceptional kindness and angelic disposition. His fame spread far and wide. The orator Libanius wrote to an Egyptian official: "You cannot surely be ignorant of Didymus, unless you are ignorant of the great city wherein he has night and day been pouring out his learning for the good of others." The tone of his writings is always well balanced and calculated to win over his opponent rather than to defeat him. He always railed against the heresy but never the heretic. Thus, he had friends even among the Arians.

Didymus was never ordained, remaining instead a layman living a life of austerity in relative isolation outside Alexandria. He has, however, never been accorded the title of saint due to Origenist opinions concerning the pre-existence of souls and the ultimate salvation of all in his writings. This unfortunate circumstance is the reason why his name appears side by side with that of Origen in the condemnation of the Third Council of Constantinople in AD 680.

His condemnation also explains why much of what Didymus composed has also been lost. His voluminous exegetical works on most of the Old and New Testament books have virtually all disappeared. So, too, his dogmatic works. Besides a few fragments discovered here and there, only two works remain — his treatise on the Holy Spirit and his three books on the Trinity. The former was extensively used by St Ambrose in his own work on the Holy Spirit and survives in St Jerome's Latin translation; the latter is Didymus' principal work and has survived intact probably due to being free of Origenism.

After a life devoted to prayer, penance and work, Didymus died peacefully in AD 398 at the age of 85. Soon after, the catechetical school of Alexandria moved to Side where it failed to meet success and closed permanently.

Extracts

The Holy Spirit (ante AD 381)

35
"God is simple and of an incomposite and spiritual nature, having neither ears nor organs of speech. A solitary essence and illimitable, He is composed of no numbers and parts. This, indeed, is likewise to be accepted in respect to the Son and the Holy Spirit."

37
"So too the Son is said to receive from the Father the very things by which He subsists. For neither has the Son anything else except those things given Him by the Father, nor has the Holy Spirit any other substance than that given Him by the Son. And on that account we do affirm those propositions according to which we believe that in the Trinity the nature of the Holy Spirit is the same as that of the Father and the Son."

The Trinity (inter AD 381-392)

2:6:7
"The creature does not participate substantially in the rational soul, as if by indwelling in it; for so to participate is proper to God alone. But the Holy

Spirit, in His subsisting, participates substantially, as do the Father and the Son ... From the very beginning of the Father's indwelling in those who are worthy, is it not of necessity, in view of the unity of the divine nature and its fullness in its indwelling in us, that the Son and the Holy Spirit join and concur in that incursion? Surely no one would ever want to say that it is as if a multiplicity of gods were indwelling in us, but one God, the three Persons subsisting quite as One in the unity of the Godhead."

3:4
"It helps us to understand the terms first-born and only-begotten when the Evangelist tells that Mary remained a virgin 'until she brought forth her first-born son'; for neither did Mary, who is to be honored and praised above all others, marry anyone, nor did she ever become the Mother of anyone else, but even after childbirth she remained always and forever an immaculate virgin."

3:12
"The saying, 'I came down from heaven, not to do My will but that of the Father who sent Me,' is to be taken in this sense: 'In the Incarnation I am not doing the will of My humanity, but that of My Divinity.' For the will of the Beloved Son is not separate from the will of God the Father. In the Trinity there is one and the same will."

Against the Manicheans (date unknown)

8 & 9
"Hence the understanding about bodies begotten in marriage; and thus, since the coming together of Adam and Eve came about after sin, the flesh is for that reason called the flesh of sin ... But when the Savior was sojourning here, just as there was a taking away of sin from other things, so too from marriage ... And in a different way it may be said even more naturally that virginity is something divine, and is accounted among the virtues. If, therefore, someone compares virginity to marriage, the latter may be called sin; but it is not sin in the absolute sense."

St Cyril of Jerusalem

(c. AD 315–386)

Historical Note

The precise time and place of St Cyril's birth are unknown but it was probably in or around Jerusalem between AD 313 and 315. St Cyril was educated in Jerusalem and was ordained a priest between AD 343 and 345 by the orthodox St Maximus and consecrated bishop of Jerusalem in AD 348 by the Arian bishop Acacius of Caesarea on condition that he renounce the ordination bestowed by St Maximus. St Cyril consented to this impiety and committed other frauds to maintain his position, but soon fell into conflict with Acacius and the Arians over the question of precedence between Caesarea and Jerusalem and his correct Christology and attachment to the Nicene formula.

Like St Athanasius, St Cyril's career as a bishop was a stormy one. Because of his anti-Arianism he was exiled from his see on three occasions – AD 357, 360, and 367. His last exile lasted twelve years, only regaining his see and finding peace after the death of the Emperor Valens and the accession of the Emperor Theodosius in AD 379. St Cyril was also questioned by orthodox Catholics for his use at times of the term *homoiosious*, though in an orthodox sense.

After AD 379, St Cyril continued unmolested as bishop of Jerusalem, participating in the Council of Constantinople in AD 381 where he unequivocally accepted the term *homoosious* and the divinity of the Holy Spirit after an alleged silence. St Cyril was neither a man of higher intellect nor an original writer. His greatest skills were those of catechist and popular preacher. For these his listeners admired him very much. He died on 18 March, AD 386.

Except for a small number of fragments of certain homilies (a sermon on the Pool of Bethesda, a letter to the Emperor Constantius and three other fragments) the only complete and genuine work of St Cyril still extant is the *Catechetical Lectures*. The lectures were probably delivered between AD 347 and 350 and number twenty-four – one introduction;

eighteen pre-baptismal discourses for catechumens; and five mystagogic discourses for neophytes. They constitute a series of explanations about the Creed catechumens were about to recite and the ceremonies of Christian initiation they were about to undergo – Baptism, Confirmation and the Eucharist. They also contain interesting references to the discovery of the True Cross, the position of Mount Calvary, and the great basilica built by Constantine. They are the most ancient methodical explanation of the Creed in our possession and therefore their importance cannot be underestimated.

The *Lectures* come down to us not from the hand of St Cyril, but as shorthand transcripts taken down from someone in his audience. Their style is clear, dignified and logical, full of seriousness and piety. Some scholars regard the last five mystagogic discourses as being rather the work of St Cyril's successor, John of Jerusalem. The most likely scenario is that they were originally composed by St Cyril and then later revised by John (Jurgens Vol. 1, p. 347; Quasten, *Patrology*, Vol. 3, pp.364-366).

Extracts

***Catechetical Lectures* (c. AD 350)**

1:5
"Cleanse your vessel that you may receive grace more abundantly; for although the remission of sins is given to all equally, the communion of the Holy Spirit is bestowed in proportion to the faith of such. If you have labored little, you will receive little; but if your labor has been great, great will be your reward ... By the loving-kindness of God you have, in our former meetings, heard enough about Baptism and Chrism, and of the reception of the Body and Blood of Christ. And now it behoves us to pass on to what is next ..."

4:11
"(Christ) descended into the subterranean regions so that He might ransom from there the just ... David was there, and Samuel, and all the Prophets; and John, the same who, through his messengers, said: 'Are You

the one who is to come, or shall we look for another?' Would you not want Him to go down to free such men as these?"

4:25
"Let those also be of good cheer who are married and use their marriage properly; who enter marriage lawfully, and not out of wantonness and unbounded license; who recognize periods of continence so that they may give themselves to prayer; who in the assemblies bring clean bodies as well as clean garments into church; who have embarked upon the matrimonial estate for the procreation of children, and not for the sake of indulgence."

4:26
"And those who are once married - let them not hold in contempt those who have accommodated themselves to a second marriage. Continence is a good and wonderful thing; but still, it is permissible to enter upon a second marriage, lest the weak might fall into fornication."

15:22
"But what - lest a hostile power dare to counterfeit it - is the sign of His coming? 'And He shall appear,' He says, 'the sign of the Son of Man in the heavens.' Christ's own true sign is the cross. The sign of a luminous cross shall go before the King, pointing out Him that was formally crucified."

18:1
"The root of every good work is the hope of the resurrection; for the expectation of a reward nerves the soul to good work. Every laborer is prepared to endure the toils if he looks forward to the reward of these toils. But they who labor without reward - their soul is exhausted with their body ... He that believes his body will remain for the resurrection is careful of his garment and does not soil it in fornication, or abuses his own body as if it belonged to another. A great precept and teaching of the Holy Catholic Church, therefore, is belief in the resurrection of the dead - great and most necessary, but contradicted by many ..."

23 (Mystagogic 5):10
"Then we make mention also of those who have already fallen asleep: first, the patriarchs, prophets, Apostles, and martyrs, that through their prayers

and supplications God would receive our petition; next, we make mention also of the holy fathers and bishops who have already fallen asleep, and, to put it simply, of all among us who have already fallen asleep; for we believe that it will be of very great benefit to the souls of those for whom the petition is carried up, while this holy and most solemn Sacrifice is laid out."

23 (Mystagogic 5):15

"Give us this day our supersubstantial bread. The bread which is of the common sort is not supersubstantial. But the Bread which is holy, that Bread is supersubstantial, as if to say, directed toward the substance of the soul. This Bread does not go into the belly, to be cast out into the privy. Rather, it is distributed through your whole system, for the benefit of body and soul."

23 (Mystagogic 5):21

"In approaching, therefore, do not come up with your wrists apart or with your fingers spread, but make of your left hand a throne for the right, since you are about to receive into it a king. And having hollowed your palm, receive the Body of Christ, saying over it 'Amen.' Then, after cautiously sanctifying your eyes by the touch of the Holy Body, partake, being careful lest you lose anything of it. For whatever you might lose is clearly a loss to you from one of your own members. Tell me: if someone gave you some grains of gold, would you not hold them with all carefulness, lest you might lose something of them and thereby suffer a loss? Will you not, therefore, be much more careful in keeping watch over what is more precious than gold and gems, so that not a particle of it may escape you?"

23 (Mystagogic 5):22

"Then, after you have communicated yourself of the Body of Christ, come forward also to the cup of His Blood, not reaching out with your hands, but bowing; and in an attitude of worship and reverence say the Amen, and sanctify yourself by partaking also of the Blood of Christ. And while the moisture of it still adheres to your lips, touch it with your hands and sanctify your eyes and forehead and the rest of your senses. Then, while awaiting the prayer, give thanks to God, who has deemed you worthy of such great Mysteries."

St Hilary of Poitiers

(c. AD 315–367/368)

Historical Note

St Hilary was the great pro-Nicene bishop of Gaul, and hence has been called the Athanasius of the West. Born of wealthy pagan parents, the young Hilary was educated in philosophy and rhetoric before marrying. Soon afterwards, he began a study of the Old and New Testaments which ultimately resulted in his conversion to Christianity.

In AD 350, due to his wide learning and zeal for the Faith the local inhabitants of Poitiers, both clergy and laity, unanimously elected St Hilary their bishop. This was despite the fact that he was married. Upon becoming Bishop, St Hilary campaigned against the Arian Metropolitan of Gaul, Saturninus of Arles, and refused to subscribe to Arian formulas put forward by the Emperor Constantius, encouraging other bishops to do likewise. This resulted in his exile to Phrygia in Asia Minor.

While in exile, St Hilary learned Greek and familiarized himself entirely with the Arian controversy. He also composed his *Commentary on the Gospel of Matthew*, the *Encyclical Letter on the Councils* and his masterpiece *The Trinity* in twelve volumes. Remaining undeterred, he continued to harass Arianism relentlessly, challenging the Arians to a debate before the Emperor and seeking to win over the Semi-Arians. He also professed his intention of challenging the most ardent Arians in their stronghold of Constantinople. The pro-Arian authorities had St Hilary sent back to Poitiers as a "disrupter of the peace of the East."

St Hilary returned to Poitiers to the wild cheers and acclamations of laity and clergy alike. He then secured the excommunication and deposition of Saturninus and rallied strayed laity and weak bishops back to the faith of Nicaea. From AD 362 to 364, he engaged in similar work in Italy in collaboration with Eusebius of Vercellae. After openly assailing the pro-Arian Auxentius, bishop of Milan, St Hilary was expelled from Italy by the Emperor Valentinian. After the deaths of the pro-Arian Emperors,

Arianism died a rapid death in the West. This was in no doubt due to the work of St Hilary.

St Hilary can be compared and contrasted with St Athanasius in many ways. Both were firm in character, noble in outlook, effective in government and prominent in doctrinal controversy. St Athanasius' career was longer and produced more action and writing, yet St Hilary possessed superior speculative thought and deeper theological penetration. Some, however, including St Jerome, criticized him for being too lofty and unsuited to the less educated and refined.

St Hilary died in Poitiers on 13 January, AD 367 or 368 and was proclaimed a Doctor of the Church by Pope Pius IX in 1851.

Extracts

Commentary on the Gospel of Matthew **(inter AD 353-355)**

4:22
"... now evangelic faith enjoins upon a husband not only a good will in respect to keeping peace, but even levels against him a charge of collusion in regard to the adultery of a wife, if she marry another out of the necessity created by her separation; and it sets forth no other cause for terminating a marital union except this: lest a man might be soiled by the company of a promiscuous wife."

18:8
"In our present condition we are all subdued by the terror of that greatest dread. And now, out in front of that terror, He sets the irrevocable apostolic judgment, however severe, so that those whom they shall bind on earth, that is, whomsoever they leave bound in the knots of their sins; and those whom they loose, which is to say, those who by their confession receive grace unto salvation: — these, in accord with the apostolic sentence, are bound or loosed also in heaven."

The Trinity (inter AD 356-359)

2:1

"Believers have always found satisfaction in that utterance of God which, by the testimony of the evangelist, was poured out into our ears with the very power of its own truth: 'Going now, teach all nations, baptizing them in the name of the Father and of the Son and of the Holy Spirit, teaching them to observe everything whatsoever I have commanded you. And behold, I am with you all days, even to the consummation of the world' ... He commanded them to baptize in the name of the Father, and of the Son, and of the Holy Spirit: that is, in a confession of the Author, and of the Only-begotten, and of the Gift."

2:29

"Concerning the Holy Spirit, however, I ought not remain silent, nor yet is it necessary to speak. Still, on account of those who do not know Him, it is not possible for me to be silent. However, it is not necessary to speak of Him who must be acknowledged, who is from the Father and the Son, His sources. Indeed, it is my opinion that there ought be no discussion about whether He exists ... I think, however, that the reason why some remain in ignorance or doubt about this, is that they see this third name, that by which the Holy Spirit is named, applied frequently also to the Father and to the Son. But there need be no objection to this, for both Father and Son are spirit and holy."

7:4

"The Church, instituted by the Lord and confirmed by the Apostles, is one for all men; but the frantic folly of the diverse impious sects has cut them off from her. It cannot be denied that this tearing asunder of the faith has arisen from the defect of poor intelligence, which twists what is read to conform to its opinion, instead of adjusting its opinion to the meaning of what is read. However, while individual parties fight among themselves, the Church stands revealed not only by her own doctrines, but by those also of her adversaries. And although they are all ranged against her, she confutes the most wicked error which they all share, by the very fact that she is alone and one."

Commentaries on the Psalms (c. AD 365)

On Ps. 54 (53)

"We have declared repeatedly and without cease that it was the only-begotten Son of God who was crucified, and that He was condemned to death: He that is eternal by reason of the nature which is His by His birth from the eternal Father; and it must be understood that He underwent the passion not from any natural necessity, but for the sake of the mystery of man's salvation; and that His submitting to the passion was not from His being compelled thereto, but of His own will ... God suffered, therefore, because He voluntarily submitted Himself to the passion."

On Ps. 130 (129)

"We recall that there are many spiritual powers, to whom the name angels is given, or presidents of Churches. There are, according to John, angels of the Churches of Asia. And there were, as Moses bears witness, when the sons of Adam were separated, bounds appointed for the peoples according to the number of the angels. And, as the Lord teaches, there are for little children, angels who see God daily. There are, as Raphael told Tobias, angels assisting before the majesty of God, and carrying to God the prayers of suppliants. Mention is made of all this, because you might wish to understand these angels as the eyes, or the ears, or the hands, or the feet of God."

St Basil the Great

(c. AD 330–379)

Historical Note

St Basil is ranked as the first of the great 'Three Cappadocians', together with his dear friend St Gregory Nazianzus and his brother St Gregory of Nyssa. Together, these three were instrumental in the triumph of the faith of Nicaea and Constantinople in the East against Arianism and its offshoots.

Born around AD 330 in Caesarea, Cappadocia, St Basil was the eldest of ten children in a very illustrious family. His father was the son of St Macrina the Elder and his mother the daughter of a martyr. Besides himself, two of St Basil's brothers also became bishops and one of his sisters a saintly model of the ascetical life.

St Basil was trained by his father in rhetoric, and later was educated in the schools of Caesarea, Constantinople and Athens. It was while in Athens that he formed his lasting friendship with St Gregory Nazianzus.

St Basil was baptized in AD 356 and afterwards journeyed throughout Egypt, the Middle East and Mesopotamia in search of a life of ascetical perfection. He, however, returned home and established his own colony of monks on the banks of the Iris River devoted to prayer, study and manual labor.

In AD 360, St Basil was forced to leave his secluded retreat and traveled to Constantinople with his bishop Dianus. Soon he became directly embroiled in the conflict against Arianism and Macedonian denials of the divinity of the Holy Spirit. It was during this time of conflict that his great gifts were noticed and appreciated, and St Basil was elevated to the see of Caesarea in AD 370. He excelled as a man of action and government. His episcopal activity was manifold: to oppose Arianism and the Emperor Valens; to win over the opponents of Nicaea; to assist in bringing peace to the Church in Antioch; and to gain the help of orthodox Catholics in the West. During the reign of Valens, St Basil was one of literally only a handful of faithful eastern bishops who held on to their sees. This he did through a combination of strength of character, courage and prudence.

Immediately after St Basil's death on 1 January, AD 379, he was hailed as "the Great." The Church has had few other men so richly gifted and talented. His intelligence, eloquence and character earned him the reputation of being "a Roman among the Greeks." Yet, his speech was always familiar and simple. Difficulties and failures never stopped or disheartened him and to the very end of his life he fought for truth and peace. It is understandable why the Eastern Church ranks him, together with St John Chrysostom, as one of its great pillars and Doctors.

St Basil's greatest works include his anti-Arian *Against Eunomius* and his anti-Macedonian *On the Holy Spirit*. He also composed numerous discourses and homilies on the Hexameron (the work of the six days of creation) and others aimed at edification, as well as hundreds of other letters and writings on miscellaneous subjects. In his ascetical works we find the first rule for monks in Asia Minor which later was to influence monasticism in the West through St Benedict. In addition, there still exists a Liturgy bearing his name which, however, has been modified over the centuries.

Extracts

Against Eunomius (inter AD 363-365)

3:1
"All the angels, having but one appellation, have likewise among themselves the same nature, even though some of them are set over nations, while others of them are guardians to each one of the faithful."

Rules Briefly Treated (post AD 370)

229
"Just as the diseases of the body are not divulged to all, nor haphazardly, but to those who are skilled in curing them, so too our declaration of our sins should be made to those empowered to cure them ..."

288
"It is necessary to confess our sins to those to whom the dispensation of God's mysteries is entrusted. Those doing penance of old are found to have done it before the saints. It is written in the Gospel that they confessed their sins to John the Baptist; but in Acts they confessed to the Apostles, by whom also all were baptized."

Letter to a Patrician Lady Caesarea (c. AD 372)

93
"To communicate each day and to partake of the holy Body and Blood of Christ is good and beneficial; for He says quite plainly: 'He that eats My Flesh and drinks My Blood has eternal life.' Who can doubt that to share continually in life is the same thing as having life abundantly? We ourselves communicate four times each week, on Sunday, Wednesday, Friday, and Saturday; and on other days if there is a commemoration of any saint."

First Letter to Amphilochius, Bishop of Iconium (AD 374)

188:2
"A woman who has deliberately destroyed a fetus must pay the penalty for murder."

188:13
"Our Fathers did not reckon killings in war as murders, but granted pardon, as it seems to me, to those who were fighting in defense of virtue and piety. Perhaps, however, they should be advised that, since their hands are not clean, they should abstain from Communion for a period of three years."

The Holy Spirit (AD 375)

12:28
"Let no one be misled by the fact that the Apostle frequently omits the name of the Father and of the Holy Spirit when mentioning baptism; nor let anyone suppose that the invocation of the Names is a matter of

indifference ... The naming of Christ, you see, is the confession of the whole; it bespeaks the God who anoints, the Son who is anointed, and the Spirit who is the anointing ... If, then, in baptism the separation of the Spirit from the Father and the Son is perilous to the one baptizing and useless to the one receiving, how can it be safe for us to separate the Spirit from the Father and the Son?"

27:66
"Of the dogmas and kerygmas preserved in the Church, some we possess from written teaching and others we receive from the tradition of the Apostles, handed on to us in mystery. In respect to piety both are of the same force. No one will contradict any of these, no one, at any rate, who is even moderately versed in matters ecclesiastical. Indeed, were we to try to reject unwritten customs as having no great authority, we would unwittingly injure the Gospel in its vitals ..."

18:45
"It does not follow that there are two kings because we speak of a king and a king's image. The authority is not split nor is the glory divided. The sovereignty and power to the authority which we are subject is one, just as the glory we ascribe thereto is not plural but one; for the honor paid to the image passes to the prototype."

On Baptism (ante AD 379)

13:5
"For prisoners, Baptism is ransom, forgiveness of debts, death of sin, regeneration of the soul, a resplendent garment, an unbreakable seal, a chariot to heaven, a protector royal, a gift of adoption."

On the Holy Generation of Christ (ante AD 379)

5
"But since the lovers of Christ (that is, the faithful) do not allow themselves to hear that the Mother of God ceased at a given moment to be a virgin, we consider their testimony to be sufficient."

St Gregory Nazianzus

(c. AD 328/29–c. 389/90)

Historical Note

St Gregory was the second of the three great Cappadocians. He was born around the years AD 328-329 nearby the town of Nazianzus. His father, also named Gregory, had been a heretic (the sect of the Hypsistarii) but after his conversion effected through his pious wife was consecrated bishop of Nazianzus.

St Gregory and St Basil became the closest of friends while studying together in Caesarea, Alexandria and Athens. Yet they were altogether different in temperament, with St Basil having a tendency towards arrogance and volatility while St Gregory was mild, gentle and sensitive. It was their true Christian friendship that perhaps kept them together despite a number of quarrels and exchanges of severe letters.

It was not until AD 360 that St Gregory was baptized. At the demand of his aging father's congregation, and to some extent against his will, St Gregory was ordained to the priesthood on Christmas AD 361. Excepting for a short stay at St Basil's monastery on the Iris River, St Gregory assisted his father in Nazianzus.

In AD 371, St Gregory was consecrated bishop of Sasima by St Basil who sought his assistance in his dispute against the Emperor Valens and the bishop of nearby Tyana. It was a miserable desert village crossroad in Cappadocia and St Gregory never took charge of it, remaining in Nazianzus assisting his father until his death in AD 374. St Gregory's abandonment of Sasima was the cause of an unhappy estrangement between him and St Basil.

St Gregory then withdrew to a retreat in Seleucia and, after hearing of St Basil's death in AD 379, was invited by the Nicene party to be their bishop in Constantinople, a long-time stronghold of the Arians. Despite his instinctive longing for solitude he accepted and in the small chapel of the *Anastasis* delivered his famous discourses on the Trinity to the beleaguered Catholic community and heretics who had come attracted by St Gregory's sanctity, learning and eloquence. He was a born orator with a clear vision and vivid imagination.

On 27 November, AD 380, the Emperor Theodosius installed St Gregory as the Archbishop of Constantinople. In this capacity he attended the First Council of Constantinople in May AD 381. However, numerous objections were raised against his elevation to the Archbishopric on the grounds that it was uncanonical to transfer a bishop from one see to another. The opposition was so great that St Gregory resigned and returned to Nazianzus, where he took charge for two years before retiring to his family estate in solitude until his death around AD 389/390.

The literary work of St Gregory comprised discourses, poems and letters — forty-five discourses, two books of poems and two hundred and forty-four letters. His writing style was ornate, refined and studied. He is one of the most admired Byzantine writers, earning the title of *Theologus*, or the Divine. The most remarkable aspect of his writing is his theological language. In his Trinitarian and Christological writings are found precise formulas which express definitively orthodox dogmas. There has been no need to refine them since.

Extracts

In Praise of Hero the Philosopher (AD 379)

25:16
"Common to Father and Son and Holy Spirit is their having no coming into being, and their divinity. Common to Son and Holy Spirit is their coming from the Father. Proper to the Father alone is His unbegottenness; to the Son alone, His begottenness; to the Spirit alone, His being sent forth."

Second Theological Oration (AD 380)

28:16
"Let us suppose that the existence of the universe is spontaneous. To what will you ascribe its order? If you like, we will grant even that. But to what then will you ascribe its preservation and its being maintained in the terms of its first existence? Something else, or is that also spontaneous? Surely to

something other than chance! But what else can this be, except God? Thus reason, which is from God and implanted in all of us, which is our first law and is participated in by all, leads us to God through the things we can see."

28:31
"We know that there are certain Angels and Archangels, Thrones, Dominations, Principalities, Powers, Splendors, Ascents, Intelligent Virtues or Intelligences, natures pure and unalloyed; immovable to evil, or so moved only with difficulty; circling ever in chorus around the First Cause."

Third Theological Oration (AD 380)

29:16
"Father is the name neither of an essence nor of an action, but of the relation which describes how the Father stands to the Son, and the Son to the Father. With us these names make known a genuine and real relation; and here too they signify an identity of nature of the Begotten to the Begetter."

Fourth Theological Oration (AD 380)

30:15
"Their tenth objection is ignorance, the statement that the final day and hour is known to none, not even the Son, except the Father. But how is it possible that Wisdom should be ignorant of any of those things that are? ... How indeed could He know so accurately those things which are to precede that hour and which are to take place at the end, but be ignorant of the hour itself ... If, then, we may proceed from the example of what is seen to what is known, is it not perfectly plain to everyone that He does know as God, but says that, as Man, He knows not?"

Against the Arians and About Myself (AD 380)

33:17
"Remember your profession of faith. In whose name were you baptized? In the Father's name? Jewish, but good. In the Son's name? Good; no longer Jewish, but not yet perfect. In the Holy Spirit's name? Excellent! This is perfect!"

On the Theophany or Birthday of Christ (AD 380)

38:13
"He was conceived by the Virgin, who had first been purified by the Spirit in soul and body; for as it was fitting that childbearing should receive its share of honor, so it was necessary that virginity should receive even greater honor."

Oration on Holy Baptism (AD 381)

40:17
"Do you have an infant child? Allow sin no opportunity; rather, let the infant be sanctified from childhood. From the most tender age let him be consecrated by the Spirit. Do you fear the seal because of the weakness of nature? O what a pusillanimous mother, and of how little faith! ... Give your child the Trinity, that great and noble protector."

40:23
"If you are able to judge a man who intends to commit murder solely by his intention and without there having been any act of murder, then you can likewise reckon as baptized one who desired Baptism without having received Baptism."

Letter to Cledonius the Priest, Against Apollinaris (AD 382)

101
"If anyone does not agree that Holy Mary is the Mother of God, he is at odds with the Godhead. If anyone asserts that Christ passed through the Virgin as through a channel, and was not shaped in her both divinely and

humanly, divinely because without man and humanly because in accord with the law of gestation, he is likewise godless ...

... But He is not two Persons! Far be it! Both are one by their conjunction, the divine made man and the human deified ...

... If anyone has hoped in Christ as a Man lacking a mind, he is truly mindless and is quite unworthy of being saved."

Letter to Amphilochius, Bishop of Iconium (c. AD 383)

171
"Cease not to pray and plead for me when you draw down the Word by your word, when in an unbloody cutting you cut the Body and Blood of the Lord, using your voice for a sword."

St Gregory of Nyssa

(c. AD 335–394)

Historical Note

St Gregory of Nyssa was the younger brother of the great St Basil and the third of the Three Cappadocians. Born around AD 335, St Gregory was educated by his older brother and destined for the Church at a young age. St Gregory was known to call his brother Basil "our father and master."

However, after advancing to the office of lector, a crisis of conscience caused St Gregory to abandon a career in the Church for a worldly career as a teacher of rhetoric. This was despite the remonstrations of St Basil. He soon after also married a woman named Theosebeia. However, due to the exhortations of St Gregory Nazianzus, St Gregory of Nyssa returned to his true vocation and may have briefly stayed at St Basil's monastery on the Iris River for a retreat.

In AD 371, St Basil, intent on consolidating his own authority as metropolitan against the Arians, consecrated his younger brother as bishop of Nyssa. Like St Gregory of Nazianzus, this ordination was virtually against St Gregory of Nyssa's will, but unlike the former he did take possession of his diocese. It was as bishop of Nyssa that St Gregory's poor skills as an administrator came to the fore, much to the frustration of St Basil who strongly criticized and blamed his younger brother, calling him naïve and clumsy.

St Gregory of Nyssa was not gifted as a leader or preacher, but rather as a mystic, dogmatic theologian and writer. He was a philosopher who strove to harmonize the faith with reason and show their true accord. In his writings, we find nearly all species of Christian literature – the exegetical, dogmatico-polemical, ascetical, discourses and letters. Of his works, the greatest are *Against Eunomius* and *The Great Catechism*.

In AD 376, the Arians falsely accused St Gregory of misappropriation of funds and persuaded the local governor of Pontus to order his arrest. St Gregory at first allowed himself to be arrested, but losing heart from the brutal treatment he received, escaped to a secret place of safety. St Gregory was then deposed as bishop in absentia by the Synod of Nyssa. He managed to regain his see two years later after the death of the Emperor Valens, and was received with joy by the local populace.

After St Basil died in AD 379, a new era of activity began for St Gregory of Nyssa. He was highly regarded by the Emperor Theodosius and his see is named in one of his edicts as a center of Catholic communion in the East. In AD 380, he was elected as Bishop of Sebaste and attended the Council of Constantinople in AD 381 where he defended St Gregory Nazianzus and was looked upon as the heir to St Basil's thought. His reputation grew to such an extent that he was chosen to preach the funeral panegyrics of the Princess Pulcheria and the Empress Flaccilla in Constantinople in AD 385.

After attending a synod at Constantinople in AD 394, St Gregory disappeared from the scene. He may have journeyed to Arabia at the behest of this Synod to repress ecclesiastical disorders there and died soon afterwards.

Extracts

Virginity (AD 370)

14
"Just as in the time of Mary, the Mother of God, the Death who had reigned from Adam until then found, when he came to her and dashed his forces against the fruit of her virginity as against a rock, that he was himself shattered against her, so too in every soul that passes through this life in flesh that is protected by virginity, the strength of Death is shattered and annulled, when Death finds no place in which to fix his sting."

Against Eunomius (inter AD 380-384)

Bk 3
"Let (Eunomius) first show, then, that the Church has believed in vain that the Only-begotten Son truly exists, not made such through adoption by a Father falsely so-called, but existing as such according to nature, by

generation from Him Who Is, not estranged from the nature of Him who begot Him ... And let no one interrupt me and say that what we confess should be confirmed by constructive reasoning. It suffices for the proof of our statement that we have a tradition coming down to us from the Fathers, an inheritance as it were, by succession from the Apostles through the saints who came after them."

Sermon on the Baptism of Christ (c. AD 383)

(Jurgens # 1062)

"The bread again is at first common bread; but when the mystery sanctifies it, it is called and actually becomes the Body of Christ. So too the mystical oil, so too the wine; if they are things of little worth before the blessing, after their sanctification by the Spirit each of them has its own superior operation. This same power of the word also makes the priest venerable and honorable, separated from the generality of men by the new blessing bestowed upon him. Yesterday he was but one of the multitude, one of the people; suddenly he is made a guide, a president, a teacher of piety, an instructor in hidden mysteries."

The Great Catechism (post AD 383)

31

"Some are saying that God, if He wanted to, could by force bring even the disinclined to accept the kerygmatic message. But then where would their free choice be? Where their virtue? Where their praise for their having succeeded? To be brought around to the purpose of another's will belongs only to creatures without a soul or irrational."

37

"Rightly then, do we believe that the bread consecrated by the word of God has been made over into the Body of God the Word. For that body was, as to its potency, bread; but it has been consecrated by the lodging there of the Word, who pitched His tent in the flesh ... not through its being eaten does it advance to become the Body of the Word, but it is made over immediately into the Body by means of the word, just as was stated by the Word, 'This is my Body!'"

The Life of Moses (c. AD 390)

2
"There is a certain opinion, having credence from its having been handed down from the Fathers, which says that when our nature fell into sin God did not leave us without protection in our misery. Rather, a certain angel from among those to whom is allotted an incorporeal nature, was appointed by Him to assist in the life of each man; but contrariwise, too, the corrupter of our nature, destructive of human life, fights against the same by the agency of a certain evil and malicious demon."

Homilies on Ecclesiastes (date unknown)

8
"Paul, joining righteousness to faith and weaving them together, constructs of them the breastplates for the infantryman, armoring the soldier properly and safely on both sides. A soldier cannot be considered safely armored when either shield is disjoined from the other. For faith without works of justice is not sufficient for salvation; neither, however, is righteous living secure in itself of salvation, if it is disjoined from faith."

The Lord's Prayer (date unknown)

Sermon 5
"'Lead us not into temptation, but deliver us from evil.' My friends, what do these words mean? It seems that the Lord gives many different names to the evil one, each suited to the difference among evil actions. So, he is devil, Beelzebub, Mammon, prince of this world, murderer of humankind, the evil one, the father of lies, and other similar names. Perhaps, in this instance, one of the names attributed to him is 'temptation.'"

St Ambrose of Milan

(c. AD 333–397)

Historical Note

St Ambrose was born in Treves, the son of the Praetorian Prefect of Gaul, probably in AD 333. His father, whose name was also Ambrose, died relatively early in life. The young Ambrose was then taken by his mother (together with his brother and sister) to Rome to receive a Christian education.

Ambrose was trained in rhetoric and law and in AD 370 was made Consul of Liguria and Emilia, with his residence in Milan. At the death of the bishop of Milan, the Arian Auxentius, there ensued much tension and violence between the Catholic and Arian factions. St Ambrose, who at the time was not even baptized, became involved in the disputes. During one of the clashes, while voices were being raised proffering different candidates for the episcopal succession, a young child began to cry out repeatedly the name of Ambrose. Immediately, the multitude, both Catholics and Arians alike, began to also call out Ambrose's name. Despite attempting to flee, St Ambrose eventually yielded to public pressure and within the space of just seven days he received the sacraments of Baptism, Confirmation, Holy Communion and Holy Orders (7 December, AD 374).

From this moment onwards, St Ambrose devoted his life to the study of the sacred sciences, the administration of his church, the care of his flock, the interests of the Empire, and the personal concerns of its rulers, namely Gratian, Valentinian II and Theodosius. St Ambrose as bishop was exemplary both in his public and private life. As a theologian, he was solely influenced by the great Fathers of the East. His strength lies in his moral and ascetical writings, which remain of great importance even today in the field of pastoral theology. He is also remembered as the author of many hymns, some of which are still recited in the Divine Office, and his name is given to the style of plainsong, Ambrosian Chant, in the liturgy of the Milanese Rite.

Publicly, St Ambrose is remembered for his successful opposition to the restoration of the statue of the Goddess of Victory to the senate chambers and his humiliation of the Emperor Theodosius for the massacre of seven thousand people at Thessalonica in AD 390. For this massacre, Theodosius was refused admittance to Milan Cathedral and ordered to do public penance. St Ambrose is considered the first of those political bishops who strove to unite Church and State for the betterment of both.

St Ambrose's extraordinary popularity was in no doubt due to his unending devotion to his flock, his dignified character and lofty views. He always catechized his people in a way that was positive and practical. The conversion of the great St Augustine was directly due to his manner, preaching and teaching. However, compared to St Augustine and even St Jerome he was a scholar of lower rank. Nevertheless, his style possessed a sweetness and harmony that always charmed St Augustine.

St Ambrose died 4 April, AD 397. The story of his life was completed by Paulinus, his intimate friend and secretary, in AD 422. It recounts many wonderful facts concerning the life of the Saint, including a number of miracles attributed to him before and after his death.

Extracts

Paradise (c. AD 375)

10:48
"Nor is it a matter of indifference that the woman was not formed of the same clay from which Adam was made, but was made from the rib of Adam himself, so that we might know that the flesh of man and woman is of but one nature, and that there is but one source of the human race. Therefore at the beginning it is not two that are made, man and woman, nor two men, nor two women, but first man is made, and then woman from him. For God willed to settle one nature upon mankind, and starting from the one origin of this creature, He snatched away the possibility of numerous and disparate natures."

The Virgins (AD 377)

2:2:6
"Mary's life should be for you a pictorial image of virginity. Her life is like a mirror reflecting the face of chastity and the form of virtue. Therein you may find a model for your own life ... showing what to improve, what to imitate, what to hold fast to."

The Widows (AD 377-378)

4:23
"There are three forms of the virtue of chastity: the first is that of spouses, the second that of widows and the third that of virgins. We do not praise any one of them to the exclusion of the others ... This is the richness of the discipline of the Church."

The Sacraments (c. AD 390-391)

4:4:14
"Who, then, is the author of the Sacraments if not the Lord Jesus? Those Sacraments came from heaven; for every counsel is from heaven."

Commentaries on Twelve of David's Psalms (inter AD 381-397)

38:25
"We saw the Prince of Priests coming to us, we saw and heard Him offering His blood for us. We follow, inasmuch as we are able, being priests; and we offer the sacrifice on behalf of the people. And even if we are of but little merit, still, in the sacrifice, we are honorable. For even if Christ is not now seen as the one who offers the sacrifice, nevertheless it is He Himself that is offered in sacrifice here on earth when the Body of Christ is offered. Indeed, to offer Himself He is made visible to us, He whose word makes holy the sacrifice that is offered."

Explanation of David the Prophet (inter AD 383-389)

1:11:56

"No conception is without iniquity, since there are no parents who have not fallen. And if there is no infant who is even one day without sin, much less can the conceptions of a mother's womb be without sin. We are conceived, therefore, in the sin of our parents, and it is in their sins that we are born."

Synodal Letter to Pope Siricius (AD 389)

42:3

"They pretend to honor marriage; but what praise can be given marriage if there is no glory in virginity? Neither do we deny that marriage has been sanctified by Christ, since the divine word says: 'The two shall become one flesh' and one spirit. But we are born before we are brought to our goal, and the mystery of the divine operation is much more excellent than the remedy for human weakness. It is quite right that a good wife be praised, but even better that a pious virgin be preferred."

Hexameron (post AD 389)

6:7:40

"But let us consider the course of our own creation. He says: 'Let Us make man to our image and to our likeness.' Who says this? Is it not God, who made you? ... To whom does He say it? Certainly not to Himself, for He does not say 'Let Me make' but 'Let Us make.' Nor to the Angels, for they are ministers; and servants can have no partnership in the operation of the master, nor works with their author. It is the Son to whom He speaks, even if the Jews will not have it and the Arians fight against it ... [And it is the Son] who is the image of God the Father, the Son who always is and who was in the beginning."

St John Chrysostom

(inter AD 344/354—407)

Historical Note

Many have acclaimed St John Chrysostom as the greatest of the Fathers, unmatched by any one except St Augustine of Hippo. Born in Antioch between AD 344 and 354 of a noble and rich family, St John in his early years was educated by his widowed mother and later studied philosophy and rhetoric in the schools of Andragathius and Libanius respectively.

At the age of eighteen, St John met and was baptized by Meletius, Bishop of Antioch, who noticed his great potential. Abandoning a brief career in law, St John then commenced studying theology and three years later was ordained lector. Afterwards, despite his mother's protests, St John left Antioch to live in solitude for four years with a hermit and then another two by himself in his own cave. The severity of St John's life during this latter period caused considerable damage to his health and he was forced to return to Antioch in AD 380. By now he was small and thin, emaciated in the face, with a wrinkled forehead and balding head.

In AD 381, St John was ordained deacon by Meletius and in AD 386 priest by Flavian. For the next twelve years St John served in the main church in Antioch and it was during this period that he acquired the name "Chrysostom" (golden-mouth) for the eloquence of his preaching. Most of his Antiochene homilies are still extant.

In AD 397, the Emperor Arcadius brought St John to Constantinople to succeed Nectarius as Bishop of that city. Though unwilling, St John received the episcopal consecration on 26 February AD 398. The honor was great but full of dangers for one determined to carry out his duty.

As Metropolitan of Constantinople, St John began a comprehensive reform of clergy and laity to combat the corruption and worldliness that infected court, monastic and city life. The joyful days of his life were over. The power of his preaching and the force of his attacks earned him many enemies, particularly the Empress Eudoxia. After deposing six bishops at the Synod of Ephesus in AD 401 for simony, all St John's enemies determined to unite to destroy him. St John also determined to put on trial his staunch enemy, Theophilus, Bishop of Alexandria, for his expulsion of forty desert monks from Egypt. Theophilus countered by convoking what became known as the Synod of the Oak, where thirty-six bishops, all enemies of St John, condemned him on twenty-nine charges and illegally declared him deposed as Bishop of Constantinople.

Under attack, St John refused to give battle and scrupled to stand up for his rights. Arcadius ordered St John exiled to Bithynia, but the fear of a popular uprising and an earthquake that rocked Constantinople that same day caused the Emperor to revoke his order. St John returned in triumph to the wild cheers of the people.

The peace was only to last two months. Again, St John was accused of preaching against the Empress. The Emperor ordered St John to retire but he refused. The Emperor then ordered the closure of his church which was secured by armed intervention on the Easter Vigil of AD 404 and after the shedding of blood.

On 9 June, AD 404, St John was exiled to Cucusus in Lesser Armenia. There he remained for three years. But his great success among the local people again aroused the hatred of his enemies who secured from the Emperor a more distant banishment to Pityus on the eastern shore of the Black Sea. It was while on route to his new place of exile, being forced to travel on foot through desert and severe weather, that St John died on 14 September, AD 407.

St John was above all a moralist and his preaching practical and popular. He wrote and preached as a father who instructs, corrects and encourages his children without reserve. No other Greek Father besides Origen has left so extensive a collection of writings as St John Chrysostom.

Extracts

On the Incomprehensible Nature of God (c. AD 386-387)

3:6

"You cannot pray at home as at church, where there is a great multitude, where exclamations are cried out to God as from one great heart, and where there is something more: the union of minds, the accord of souls, the bond of charity, the prayers of the priests."

The Priesthood (AD 387)

3:5:195

"... the latter often save the sick and perishing soul – sometimes by imposing a lighter penance, sometimes by preventing the fall. Priests accomplish this not only by teaching and admonishing, but also by the help of prayer. Not only at the time of our regeneration (in baptism), but even afterward, they have authority to forgive sins. 'Is there anyone among you sick? Let him call in the priests of the church, and let them pray over him, anointing him with oil in the name of the Lord. And the prayer of faith shall save the sick man, and the Lord shall raise him up, and if he have committed sins, he shall be forgiven.'"

Homilies on the Gospel of St Matthew (c. AD 390)

1

"Joseph did not know her, until she gave birth, being unaware of her dignity: but after she had given birth, then did he know her (by way of acquaintance). Because by reason of her child she surpassed the whole world in beauty and dignity: Since she alone in the narrow abode of her womb received him whom the world cannot contain."

19:5

"For he did not say 'thy will be done in me or in us,' but 'on earth,' the whole earth, so that error may be banished from it, truth take root in it, all vice be destroyed on it, virtue flourish on it, and earth no longer differ from heaven."

Homilies on First Corinthians (c. AD 392)

41:5
"Let us help and commemorate them. If Job's sons were purified by their father's sacrifice, why would we doubt that our offerings for the dead bring them some consolation? Let us not hesitate to help those who have died and to offer our prayers for them."

Virginity (c. AD 392)

10
"That virginity is good I do agree. But that it is even better than marriage, this I do confess and if you wish, I will add that it is as much better than marriage as heaven is better than earth, as much better as the angels are better than men. And if there were any other way in which I could say it even more emphatically, I would do so."

Homilies on the First Epistle to Timothy (inter AD 392-397)

6
"... priests are the Fathers of all, it is their duty to attend to all their spiritual children, edifying them first by a holy life, and afterwards by salutary instructions."

Homily on Galatians (inter AD 393-397)

1:18
"... He says, 'to visit Peter;' he does not say to see (heiden), but to visit and survey (historesai), a word which those, who seek to become acquainted with great and splendid cities, apply to themselves. Worthy of such trouble did he consider the very sight of Peter; and this appears from the Acts of the Apostles also."

St John Chrysostom

Homily on 2 Thessalonians (c. AD 400)

4:2
"'Therefore, brethren, stand fast and hold the traditions which you have been taught, whether by word or by our letter.' From this it is clear that they did not hand down everything by letter, but there was much also that was not written. Like that which was written, the unwritten too is worthy of belief. So let us regard the tradition of the Church also as worthy of belief. Is it a tradition? Seek no further."

St Jerome

(c. AD 342–419/420)

Historical Note

St Jerome was born Eusebius Hieronymus in Stridon, northern Dalmatia, around the year AD 342 of Christian parents. He came to Rome at the age of twenty to complete his education and had the famous grammarian Aelius Donatus as one of his teachers. He passionately devoted himself to his studies and it was while a student that he became acquainted with Rufinus of Aquileia.

As a youth St Jerome did not escape temptation but renounced his sins and was baptized by Pope Liberius c. AD 364. In his early twenties, St Jerome went to France and lived with a community of monks, first in Treves and then in Aquileia. After a few years, he set out for Jerusalem but due to ill health he cut short his journey and remained in Antioch. It was there that he began his studies of Greek. Between AD 375 and 378, he lived as a hermit in the desert of Chalcis to the east of Antioch. During these years he acquired a mastery of Hebrew and earned the reputation as a trilingual scholar. He also knew some Aramaic.

After being ordained to the priesthood in AD 379, St Jerome traveled to Constantinople where he met and became friends with Sts. Gregory Nazianzus and Gregory of Nyssa. In Constantinople, St Jerome became an admirer of the commentaries of Origen and began translations of some of his works.

In AD 382, St Jerome was invited together with Paulinus of Antioch and St Epiphanius of Salamis to Rome by Pope Damasus to attend a Synod aimed at healing the Antiochian schism. Afterwards, he remained as Damasus' secretary and confidant. It was at the commission of Damasus that St Jerome began his monumental thirty-five year project of studying and translating the Latin Scriptures.

While in Rome, St Jerome also formed and led a group of noble women who lived the ascetical life in the house of Marcella. Due to what was viewed as an imprudent relationship with these ladies, the boldness of his Scriptural criticism and his sharp criticisms of lax Roman clergymen, St Jerome developed many personal enmities. Shortly after the death of Damasus in AD 384, St Jerome and two of his female followers (Paula and Julia Eustochium) left for Jerusalem. There, he established three monasteries, one for men and two for women. St Jerome ruled over the monastery for men, Paula and Julia over the female convents.

St Jerome was first and foremost a scholar both of Christian and profane literature. His work on the Scriptures is without rival in the West. However, St Jerome was a tempestuous man who lived in tempestuous times. The Empire in his time was being strained and ravaged by the various migrating tribes; controversies raged over Origenism, Pelagianism and personally with Rufinus, Jovinian and Vigilantius. St Jerome suffered from being irascible, sarcastic and arrogant. It has been said, "Jerome, upon arriving at the heavenly portals, immediately involved St Peter in a caustic argument over Origen and the latter's orthodoxy or lack thereof. Should that have been the case, the only thing certain is that Jerome will have accounted himself the winner with the right to audit Peter's books" (Jurgens vol. 2, p. 183).

In his last years, St Jerome suffered from sickness, poverty and the death of his friends. He died in Bethlehem on 30 September, AD 419/20.

Extracts

***Letter to Pope Damasus* (inter AD 374-379)**

15:2
"I speak with the successor of the fisherman ... Though I acknowledge none as first except Christ, I am joined in communion with your Holiness, that is to say, in communion with the Chair of Peter. I know that it is upon that rock that the Church has been built. Whoever eats the Lamb outside this house is profane."

***Against Helvidius* (c. AD 383)**

17 & 18
"I now ask to which class you consider the Lord's brethren in the Gospel must be assigned. They are brethren by nature, you say. But Scripture does

not say so; it calls them neither sons of Mary, nor of Joseph. Shall we say they are brethren by race? ... The only alternative is to adopt the previous explanation and understand them to be called brethren in virtue of the bond of kindred, not of love and sympathy, nor by prerogative of race, nor yet by nature ... It is clear that our Lord's brethren bore the name in the same way that Joseph was called his father."

To Eustochium (AD 384)

Ep. 32
"Some, when they find themselves with child through their sin, use drugs to procure abortion, and when (as often happens) they die with their offspring, they enter the lower world laden with the guilt not only of adultery against Christ but also of suicide and child murder."

Commentaries on the Epistle to the Galatians (c. AD 386-387)

2:3:11
"'But since in the Law no one is justified before God, it is evident that the just man lives by faith' ... It should be noted that he does not say that a man, a person, lives by faith, lest it be thought that he is contemning good works. Rather, he says the just man lives by faith. He implies thereby that whoever would be faithful and would conduct his life according to the faith can in no other way arrive at the faith or live in it except first he be a just man of pure life, coming up to the faith as it were by certain degrees."

Commentaries on Ecclesiastes (c. AD 388-389)

4:4
"If the serpent, the devil, bites someone secretly, he infects that person with the venom of sin. And if the one who has been bitten keeps silence and does not do penance, and does not want to confess his wound to his brother and to his master, who have the word that will cure him, cannot very well assist him. For if the sick man is ashamed to confess his wound to the physician, medicine will not cure that to which it is not applied."

On the Three Solomonic Books (c. AD 398)

Preface

"There is also the book of Jesus, son of Sirach ... and another book, Wisdom, attributed to Solomon ... the second was never known in Hebrew, for its very style bespeaks Greek eloquence; and some of the older authors affirm that it is a work of Philo the Jew. Just as the Church reads Judith and Tobias and the Books of Maccabees, but does not accept them as belonging among the canonical Scriptures, so too let her read these two volumes for the edification of the people but not for the purpose of confirming the authority of the Church's teachings."

Against Vigilantius (AD 406)

6

"You say in your book that while we live we are able to pray for each other, but afterwards when we have died, the prayer of no person for another can be heard; and this is especially clear since the martyrs, though they cry vengeance for their own blood, have never been able to obtain their request. But if the Apostles and martyrs while still in the body can pray for others, at a time when they ought still be solicitous about themselves, how much more will they do so after their crowns, victories, and triumphs."

Commentary on the Psalms (ante AD 420)

Ps. 44

"'The Queen stood on the right hand in gilded clothing, surrounded with variety' (Ps. 44:10). We read how the angels have come to the death and burial of some of the saints, and how they have accompanied the souls of the elect to heaven with hymns and praises. How much more should we believe that the heavenly army, with all its bands, came forth rejoicing in festal array, to meet the Mother of God, surrounded with her effulgent light, and led her with praises and canticles to the throne prepared for her from the beginning of the world."

St Augustine of Hippo

(AD 354–430)

Historical Note

Of all the Fathers of the Church, the greatest of all is St Augustine of Hippo. Jurgens makes the poignant comment, *"If we were faced with the unlikely proposition of having to destroy completely either the works of Augustine or the works of all the other Fathers and Writers, I have little doubt that all the others would have to be sacrificed. Augustine will remain"* (Vol. 3, p. 1). No other Father wrote so well as St Augustine, and no other has been written about so much.

Born in the insignificant town of Tagaste in Numidia on 13 November, AD 354, Aurelius Augustinus was born of a pagan father and Christian mother. His father, Patricius, converted to Christianity in the fourteenth year of his marriage. His mother was the ever-famous model of motherhood and virtue, St Monica.

Always extraordinarily gifted and talented, St Augustine left for Carthage at the age of seventeen to further his studies. However, it was in Carthage that he fell into a dissolute lifestyle and entered an irregular sixteen year relationship with a concubine. From this relationship was born his son, Adeodatus.

Although St Augustine was a catechumen in his early years his baptism had been postponed due to illness. In AD 374, he joined the sect of the Manichees where he remained for the next nine years. During these wayward years, St Monica continued to pray for her son's conversion. On one occasion while speaking to a bishop about how she feared for her son's salvation the bishop replied, "It is impossible that the son of these tears should perish."

Always searching for the truth, St Augustine abandoned Manicheism when confronted with the ignorance of its supposed champion, Faustus of Milevis. In AD 383, St Augustine obtained a teaching position in rhetoric in Milan through the offices of the prefect Symmachus. It was while there that he came into contact with St Ambrose and his preaching. It was St Ambrose who played the proximate role in St Augustine's conversion. The decision to convert came in August AD 386. In April, AD 387, in the presence of his mother and son, St Augustine received baptism at the hands of St Ambrose. Only a few months later, St Monica was to die after sharing the famous ecstasy of Ostia with her now converted son.

One must never underestimate the role of St Monica. For sixteen years she persevered in prayer for her son's conversion to Catholicism and the regulation of his relationship. But even she had no idea that her perseverance would bring forth not only a conversion, but also a bishop, a confessor and defender of the Faith, a Father and Doctor of the Church and foremost above all, a Saint.

After his mother's death, St Augustine returned to Africa. Three years of monastic life in Tagaste (during which Adeodatus died) was followed by ordination to the priesthood in AD 391. In AD 395, St Augustine was consecrated co-bishop of Hippo by Bishop Valerius. A year later he was bishop of Hippo in his own right.

As bishop, besides the daily duties of administering his diocese, directing his clergy, and instructing and sanctifying his people, St Augustine used his pen to author the largest surviving Patristic corpus of letters and sermons. His *Confessions* and *The City of God* will always remain two of the greatest literary treasures of Christianity. His *De Trinitate* is the most important of his dogmatic works. He also authored a Rule for religious life and combated all the major heresies of his day, in particular Manicheism, Arianism, Donatism and Pelagianism. He also dealt with exegesis, mathematics, aesthetics, music, grammar and poetry.

The invasion of the Vandals marked the end of his prolific life and works. St Augustine died in Hippo on 28 August, AD 430, while the barbarians lay siege to the city.

Extracts

Sermons (inter AD 391-430)

57:7

"The Eucharist is our daily bread. The power belonging to this divine food makes it a bond of union. Its effect is then understood as unity, so that, gathered into his Body and made members of him, we may become what we receive ... This also is our daily bread: the readings you hear each day in church and the hymns you hear and sing. All these are necessities for our pilgrimage."

Hymn Against the Donatists (AD 393)

18

"Run through the list of those priests who have occupied the See of Peter Himself; and in that list of Fathers, see who succeeded to whom. This is the Rock which the proud Gates of Hell do not overcome."

Against the Letter of Mani (AD 397)

5:6

"If you should find someone who does not yet believe in the Gospel, what would you answer him when he says: 'I do not believe?' Indeed, I would not believe in the Gospel myself if the authority of the Catholic Church did not influence me to do so."

Baptism (AD 400)

3:10:13

"It is one thing not to have something, and another to have it not by right or to usurp it illicitly. It is not that they are not the Sacraments of Christ and of the Church because they are used illicitly, and this not by heretics only, but by all the wicked and impious. Such persons ought to be corrected and punished, but the Sacraments should be acknowledged and revered."

Confessions (AD 400)

Bk 3:8
"Those foul offenses that are against nature should be everywhere and at all times detested and punished, such as were those of the people of Sodom, which should all nations commit, they should all stand guilty of the same crime, by the law of God, which hath not so made men that they should so abuse one another. For even that very intercourse which should be between God and us is violated, when that same nature, of which He is the Author, is polluted by the perversity of lust."

Bk 9:2
St Augustine's mother, St Monica, on her death-bed said to him: "This one request I make of you, that, wherever you be, you remember me at the Lord's altar."

Explanation of the Psalms (inter AD 392-418)

33:1
"'And he was carried in his own hands.' But, brethren, how is it possible for a man to do this? Who can understand it? Who is it that is carried in his own hands? A man can be carried in the hands of another; but no one can be carried in his own hands. How this should be understood literally of David, we cannot discover; but we can discover how it is meant of Christ. For Christ was carried in His own hands, when, referring to His own Body, He said: 'This is My Body' for He carried that Body in His hands."

98:9
"He took flesh from the flesh of Mary. He walked here in the same flesh, and gave us the same flesh to be eaten unto salvation. But no one eats that flesh unless first he adores it ... and not only do we not sin by adoring, we do sin by not adoring."

120:4
"It is no great thing to believe that Christ died. This the pagans, Jews, and all the wicked believe; in a word, all believe that Christ died. But that He

rose from the dead is the belief of Christians. To believe that He rose again, this we deem of great moment."

Letter to Januarius (c. AD 400)

54:1:1
"But in regard to those observances which we carefully attend and which the whole world keeps, and which derive not from Scripture but from Tradition, we are given to understand that they are recommended and ordained to be kept, either by the Apostles themselves or by plenary councils, the authority of which is quite vital in the Church."

Against Faustus the Manichean (c. AD 400)

20:21
"A Christian people celebrates together in religious solemnity the memorials of the martyrs, both to encourage their being imitated and so that it can share in their merits and be aided by their prayers. But it is done in such a way that our altars are not set up to any one of the martyrs, – although in their memory, – but to God Himself, the God of those martyrs ... That worship, which the Greeks call Latria and for which there is in Latin no single term, and which is expressive of the subjection owed to Divinity alone, we neither accord nor teach that it should be accorded to any save to the one God."

On the Good of Marriage (AD 401)

24
"These are the goods because of which marriages are considered good: children, fidelity, and sacrament ... The good of marriage among all nations and among all men consists in the cause of generation and the fidelity of chastity. When there is question of the people of God, however, another good can also be found: the sanctity or sacredness of the sacrament."

Letter to Boniface, A Bishop (AD 408)

98:9
"Was not Christ immolated only once in His very Person? In the Sacrament, nevertheless, He is immolated for the people not only on every Easter Solemnity but on every day; and a man would not be lying if, when asked, he were to reply that Christ is being immolated. For if the Sacraments had not a likeness to those things of which they are Sacraments, they would not be Sacraments at all; and they generally take the names of those same things by reason of this likeness."

To Proba (AD 412)

Ep. 130:12
"The Lord's Prayer is the most perfect of prayers, because if we pray aright we can say naught else save what is set down in that Prayer. For Prayer is in some sort the expression before God of our desires; consequently we can only rightly ask in our prayers for what we can rightly desire. Now in the Lord's Prayer we not only find all the petitions that we can rightly desire to make, but they are set down in the very order in which we ought to desire them, so that this Prayer not only teaches us how to ask but serves as a guide to all our desires."

Nature and Grace (AD 415)

36:42
"With the exception therefore of the Holy Virgin Mary, in whose case, out of respect for the Lord, I do not wish there to be any further question as far as sin is concerned, since how can we know what great abundance of grace was conferred on her to conquer sin in every way, seeing that she merited to conceive and bear him who certainly had no sin at all?"

The City of God Against the Pagans (inter AD 410-427)

Bk 10 (ante AD 417)
"The homage due to man, of which the Apostle spoke when he commanded servants to obey their masters, and which in Greek is called

dulia, is distinct from Latria, which denotes the homage that consists in the worship of God."

Bk 20, Ch. 9 (ante AD 427)
"Neither are the souls of the pious dead separated from the Church which even now is the Kingdom of Christ. Otherwise there would be no remembrance of them at the altar of God in the communion of the Body of Christ."

Against the Pelagians (AD 420)

4:10:27
"Now let us see the third point which, in the Pelagians, is no less shocking to Christ's every member and to His whole body. They contend that in this life there are or have been righteous men having no sin at all. By this presumption they most clearly contradict the Lord's Prayer, in which all the members of Christ cry aloud with true heart these words to be said each day: 'Forgive us our debts.'"

Adulterous Marriages (AD 419 aut 420)

50:2
"For a woman is bound as long as her husband is alive. As a consequence, therefore, the husband is also bound as long as the wife is alive. This bond renders any further union impossible without the implication of adultery. Hence four adulterers are produced of necessity from the two marriages whenever the wife remarries and the husband marries an adulteress."

The Annunciation of the Lord (date unknown)

3
"It is written (Ezek. 44:2): 'This gate shall be shut, it shall not be opened, and no man shall pass through it. Because the Lord the God of Israel hath entered in by it ...' What means this closed gate in the house of the Lord, except that Mary is to be ever inviolate? What does it mean that 'no man shall pass through it,' save that Joseph shall not know her? And what is this — 'The Lord alone enters in and goeth out by it,' except that the Holy

Ghost shall impregnate her, and that the Lord of Angels shall be born of her? And what means this — 'It shall be shut for evermore,' but that Mary is a Virgin before His birth, a Virgin in His birth, and a Virgin after His birth."

Homilies on John (AD 416 *et* 417)

11:3
"If we should say to a catechumen: 'Do you believe in Christ,' he will answer, 'I do believe,' and he will sign himself. He already carries the cross of Christ on his forehead, and he is not ashamed of the cross of the Lord."

The Care of the Dead (AD 421)

15:18
"The spirits of the dead are able to know some things which happen here, which it is necessary for them to know. And those for whom it is necessary that something be known, not only the present or the past but even the future, — they know these things by the revealing Spirit of God, just as not all men but the Prophets, while they lived, knew not all things but those which the providence of God judged ought to be revealed to them."

Enchiridion of Faith, Hope & Love (AD 421)

29:112
"In vain, therefore, do some men, indeed, very many, because of human sentiment, bewail the eternal punishment, of the damned and their perpetual, unending torments, without really believing that it shall be so ... But let them suppose, if it pleases them, that the punishments of the damned are, at certain periods of time, somewhat mitigated. For even thus it can be understood that they remain in the wrath of God that is, in damnation itself, for it is this that is called the Wrath of God, not some disturbance in the divine mind: that in His wrath, that is, by their abiding in His wrath, He does not shut up His mercies; yet He does not put an end to their eternal punishment, but only applies or interposes some relief to their torments."

Sermon Against the Jews (post AD 425)

9:13

"'From the rising of the sun even to its setting My name is great among the Gentiles, and in every place sacrifice is offered to My name, a clean oblation; for My name is great among the Gentiles, says the Lord Almighty.' What do you answer to that? Open your eyes at last, then, any time, and see, from the rising of the sun to its setting, the sacrifice of Christians is offered, not in one place only, as was established with you Jews, but everywhere; and not to just any god at all, but to Him who foretold it, the God of Israel ... Not in one place, as was prescribed for you in the earthly Jerusalem, but in every place, even in Jerusalem herself. Not according to the order of Aaron, but according to the order of Melchizedek."

Heresies (AD 428)

82

"He (Jovinian) destroyed the virginity of Mary, saying that it was lost by her parturition. He equated the merits of chaste spouses and of the faithful with the virginity of consecrated women and the continence of the male sex in holy persons choosing a celibate life."

St Cyril of Alexandria

(inter AD 370-375—444)

Historical Note

Not much is known of the early life of St Cyril of Alexandria except that he received a Christian education in his childhood and spent some time in the Egyptian desert with a community of monks.

St Cyril succeeded his uncle, the proud and cupiditous Theophilus, to the Patriarchate of Alexandria in AD 412. His candidature had been strongly opposed by those who feared that the nephew was of the same spirit as the uncle. To some extent this was true. St Cyril shared many of his uncle's attitudes and prejudices, including opposition to St John Chrysostom, whom he helped to depose at the Synod of the Oak in AD 403. (Only in AD 417 did St Cyril restore the name of Chrysostom to the diptychs of the Alexandrian Church). He also shared his uncle's ruthlessness towards heretics and Jews, punishing them with expulsion and confiscation of their places of worship. His example of ruthlessness is said by some to have inspired a Christian mob to publicly strip and murder the female pagan philosopher Hypatia for allegedly having incensed the city's Governor against the bishop.

St Cyril's ruthlessness is also evident in the great controversy that marked his time, the Nestorian heresy. That Nestorius' teachings had to be opposed and condemned is without question, but a more kind and temperate attitude on the part of St Cyril to Nestorius himself and his powerful supporters such as John of Antioch might have prevented an enduring heresy and schism.

Almost immediately after Nestorius began preaching his heresy against the hypostatic union and the term *Theotokos* St Cyril refuted him, demanded a retraction and appealed to Pope Celestine when none was forthcoming. St Cyril presided over the Council of Ephesus as vicegerent of the Pope which in its first session condemned, deposed and excommunicated Nestorius on 22 June, AD 431. Some argue that Nestorius was condemned before he even arrived in Ephesus. Nevertheless, when given the opportunity to defend his teachings he remained obstinate in his error. Defending the decrees of the Council of Ephesus even in the face of imperial opposition and imprisonment became thereafter St Cyril's life work. John of Antioch and his supporters were reconciled in AD 433, while Nestorius died miserable and impenitent in his place of exile in the deserts of Upper Egypt.

St Cyril was a prolific writer and a thorough theologian. He possessed great penetration and force in his thinking which earned him wide influence and recognition as an official authority. Pope Celestine called him "The generous defender of the Church and faith, the Catholic Doctor, and an apostolic man." He made it a rule never to promote a doctrine that he had not learned from the ancient Fathers. Though much has been lost, his extant works, which include the exegetical, the apologetical, the dogmatic, homilies and letters, still comprise ten volumes.

St Cyril died a pious death on 28 June, AD 444. He is affectionately known as *Kerlos* and proclaimed throughout the East as "Doctor of the World."

Extracts

Worship and Adoration in Spirit and in Truth (inter AD 412-429)

6
"But you, if some part of your body is suffering, and you really believe that saying the words 'Lord Sabaoth!' or some such appellation which divine Scripture attributes to God in respect to this nature has the power to drive that evil from you, go ahead and pronounce those words, making them a prayer for yourself ... I recall also the saying in the divinely inspired Scripture: 'Is anyone among you ill? Let him call in the Presbyters of the Church ... and if he be in sins they shall be forgiven him.'"

Treasury of the Holy Trinity (inter AD 423-425)

Thesis 34
"Since the Holy Spirit when He is in us effects our being conformed to God, and He actually proceeds from the Father and Son, it is abundantly

clear that He is of the divine essence, in it in essence and proceeding from it."

Commentary on the Psalms (ante AD 429)

On Ps. 113B (115):16
"... if we make images of pious men it is not so that we might adore them as gods but that when we see them we might be prompted to imitate them; and if we make images of Christ, it is so that our minds might wing aloft in yearning for Him."

Polished Comments (ante AD 429)

1:2
"Although the intention of those who worship idols, of discerning perhaps who is the maker of the universe, is corrupt and false, nevertheless, an innate and necessary law is operative therein and spontaneous knowledge does stir up the need to conceive of something more excellent and incomparably better than ourselves, which is God."

Commentary on the Twelve Minor Prophets (ante AD 429)

Joel, section 32
"The living water of holy Baptism is given to us as if in rain, and the Bread of Life as if in wheat, and the Blood as if in wine. In addition to this there is also the use of oil, reckoned as perfecting those who have been justified in Christ through holy baptism."

Commentary on Matthew (post AD 428)

On 26:27
"He states demonstratively: 'This is My Body,' and 'This is My Blood,' lest you might suppose the things that are seen are a figure. Rather, by some secret of the all-powerful God the things seen are transformed into the Body and Blood of Christ, truly offered in a sacrifice in which we, as participants, receive the life-giving and sanctifying power of Christ."

The Twelve Anathemas (AD 430)

1 & 2

"If anyone does not confess that the Emmanuel is in truth God, and that the Holy Virgin is Mother of God, because she bore according to the flesh of the Word of God when He became flesh: let him be anathema";

"If anyone does not confess that the Word of God the Father is united hypostatically to the flesh, and that Christ with His own flesh is one, that is to say, the same one is God and Man at the same time: let him be anathema."

Scholia on the Incarnation of the Only-Begotten (post AD 431)

26

"The Word, then, was God, and He became also Man; and since He was born according to the flesh for the sake of mankind, it is necessary that she who bore Him is the Mother of God. For if she did not bear God, neither is He that was born of her to be called God. If the divinely inspired Scriptures name Him God, as God having been made man and incarnate, He could not become Man in any other way than through birth from a woman: how then should she who bore Him not be the Mother of God?"

Against the Anthropomorphites (post AD 441)

16

"The Divine Scripture says that the judgment is to take place after the resurrection of the dead. But the resurrection is not to take place until Christ returns to us from heaven in the glory of the Father with the holy angels ... Since, therefore, Christ the Savior of all has not yet come down from heaven, neither has the resurrection taken place, nor has compensatory action been visited upon any ... so that those who possess the wealth of this world might know that if they do not wish to be liberal and generous and social, and choose to come to assist the needs of the poor, they will be overtaken by a terrible and inevitable punishment."

Against those who do not wish to confess that the Holy Virgin is the Mother of God (Date Unknown)

4

"Jesus did not first come into being as a simple man, before the union and communion of God in Him; but the Word Himself, coming into the Blessed Virgin herself, assumed for Himself His own temple from the substance of the Virgin, and came forth from her a man in all that could be externally discerned, while interiorly He was true God. Therefore He kept His Mother a virgin even after her child-bearing, which was done for none of the other saints."

Appendix:

Fathers of the Church

Greek

St Anastasius Sinaita (+700)
St Andrew of Crete (+740)
Aphraates (+4th century)
St Archelaus (+282)
St Athanasius (+373)
Athenagoras (+2nd century)
St Basil the Great (+379)
St Caesarius of Nazianzus (+369)
Clement of Alexandria (+215)
Pope St Clement I of Rome (+97)
St Cyril of Alexandria (+444)
St Cyril of Jerusalem (+386)
Didymus the Blind (+c. 398)
Diodore of Tarsus (+392)
St Dionysius the Great (+c. 264)
St Epiphanius (+403)
Eusebius of Caesarea (+340)
St Eustathius of Antioch (+4th cent.)
St Firmillian (+268)
Gennadius I of Constantinople (+5th cent.)
St Germanus (+732)
St Gregory of Nazianzus (+390)
St Gregory of Nyssa (+395)
St Gregory Thaumaturgus (+268)
Hermas (+2nd Century)
St Hippolytus (+236)
St Ignatius of Antioch (+c. 110)
St Isidore of Pelusium (+c. 450)
St John Chrysostom (+407)
St John Climacus (+649)

Latin

St Ambrose of Milan (+397)
Arnobius (+330)
St Augustine of Hippo (+430)
St Benedict of Nursia (+550)
St Caesarius of Arles (+542)
St John Cassian (+435)
Pope St Celestine I (+432)
Pope St Cornelius (+253)
St Cyprian of Carthage (+258)
Pope St Damasus I (+384)
Pope St Dionysius (+268)
St Ennodius (+521)
St Eucherius of Lyons (+450)
St Fulgentius (+533)
St Gregory of Elvira (+c. 392)
Pope St Gregory the Great (+604)
St Hilary of Poitiers (+367)
Pope St Innocent I (+417)
St Irenaeus of Lyons (+c. 202)
St Isidore of Seville (+636)
St Jerome (+420)
Lactantius (+323)
Pope St Leo the Great (+461)
Marius Mercator (+451)
Marius Victorinus (+4th cent.)
Minucius Felix (+2nd century)
Novatian (+257)
St Optatus (+4th century)
St Pacian (+390)
St Pamphilus (+309)

St John Damascene (+749)
Pope St Julius I (+352)
St Justin Martyr (+165)
St Leontius of Byzantium (+6th cent.)
St Macarius (+c. 390)
St Maximus the Confessor (+662)
St Melito of Sardes (+c. 180)
St Methodius of Olympus (+311)
St Nilus the Elder (+c. 430)
St Polycarp (+c. 155)
Pseudo-Dionysius the Areopagite (+6th cent.)
St Serapion (+c. 370)
St Sophronius (+638)
Tatian the Syrian (+2nd century)
Theodore of Mopsuestia (+428)
Theodoret of Cyrrhus (+c. 458)
St Theophilus of Antioch (+2nd cent.)

St Paulinus of Nola (+431)
St Peter Chrysologus (+450)
St Phoebadius Agen (+4th cent.)
St Rufinus of Aquileia (+410)
Salvian (+5th century)
Pope St Siricius (+399)
Tertullian (+222)
St Vincent of Lerins (+c. 450)
Origen (+254)
St Proclus (+c. 446)

Acknowledgments

Scripture quotes extracted from the *Revised Standard Version of the Bible (Catholic Edition)*, copyright © 1946, 1952 and 1971.

Andrew Louth, *Early Christian Writers*, Penguin Books, 1968.

Extracts from *The Faith of the Early Fathers*, Rev. William A. Jurgens, Copyright © 1970 by The Order of St Benedict, Inc. Published by The Liturgical Press, Collegeville, Minnesota.

Stephen K. Ray, *Crossing the Tiber*, (Ignatius Press, 1997 Ed.).

Tixeront-Raemers, *A Handbook of Patrology* B. Herder Book Co., 1946.

About the Author

Robert M. Haddad holds qualifications in law, theology, philosophy and religious education, namely, a LL.B (USyd.), Grad. Cert. in RE (Charles Sturt Uni.), Grad. Dip. Ed. (ACU), Grad. Dip. in Teacher Ed. (College of Teachers, London), AMLP (Oxon.), MA Theo. Studies (UNDA – University Medalist), MRelEd (UNDA) and a M. Phil (ACU). For his M. Phil. Robert researched the apologetical arguments of St Justin Martyr.

In addition to his studies, Robert has also authored various books, including *Lord of History Series* (2 volumes), *Law and Life*, *The Family and Human Life*, *Defend the Faith!*, *The Case for Christianity – St Justin Martyr's Arguments for Religious Liberty and Judicial Justice*, *Answering the Anti-Catholic Challenge* (ch. 3) and *1001 Reasons Why it's Great to be Catholic!*

From 1990-2005, Robert worked full-time at St Charbel's College, Sydney, teaching Religion and History. He held the positions of Year Co-ordinator and Religious Education Co-ordinator concurrently for ten years and was Assistant Principal (Welfare) for six years.

From 2006-2008, Robert worked full-time as the Convener of the Catholic Chaplaincy at the University of Sydney. He was also a lecturer at the Center for Thomistic Studies for eleven years (1996-2008), teaching Apologetics, Church Fathers and Church History, as well as assisting part-time with *Lumen Verum Apologetics* (1996-present) and the Catholic Adult Education Centre (2010-2013).

From 2009-2012, Robert was the Director of the Confraternity of Christian Doctrine (Sydney) and in that capacity was the chief editor of the revised *Christ our Light and Life* (3rd Edition) religious education K-12 curriculum used by Catholic students in state schools as well as the *Gratia Series* sacramental programs for children preparing for Reconciliation, First Holy Communion, and Confirmation in the Archdiocese of Sydney. He has recently also edited a new RCIA resource for use in Catholic schools in the same Archdiocese entitled *Initiate*.

In 2014, Robert was awarded an Australia Day Award by the Australia Day Council of New South Wales for his overall contribution to education. Currently, he is the Head of New Evangelization for the Catholic Education Office (Sydney) and lectures/tutors in Theology at the University of Notre Dame, Sydney. From time to time Robert also appears on the Telepace Television Network and Voice of Charity radio.

Other Works by the Author

A Seat at the Supper (General Editor; author Frank Colyer, self-published, 2001)

Introduction to Early Church History (Parousia Media, 2002)

The Apostles' Creed (Parousia Media, 2004)

Law and Life (Parousia Media, 2004)

The Case for Christianity – St Justin Martyr's Arguments for Religious Liberty and Judicial Justice (Connor Court Publishing, 2009)

The Family and Human Life (2nd Ed. co-authored with Bernard Toutounji, Parousia Media, 2011)

Defend the Faith! (Parousia Media, 2012)

Answering the Anti-Catholic Challenge (General Editor and author of ch. 3, Modotti Press, 2012)

1001 Reasons Why it's Great to be Catholic! (Parousia Media, 2014)

Christ our Light and Life (General Editor 3rd Edition, 2012) religious education curriculum K-12 used by Catholic students in government schools throughout the state of New South Wales.

Gratia Series (General Editor, 2012) sacramental programs for children preparing for Reconciliation, First Holy Communion, and Confirmation in the Archdiocese of Sydney.

Initiate (General Editor, CEO Sydney Publications, 2014), a RCIA resource for use in Catholic schools in the Archdiocese of Sydney.

www.ingramcontent.com/pod-product-compliance
Lightning Source LLC
Chambersburg PA
CBHW070109120526
44588CB00032B/1403